June 16 - August 28, 2011—Los Angeles Contemporary Exhibitions

SPECULATIVE

SPECULATIVE, an exhibition curated by Zach Blas & Christopher O'Leary
June 16 - August 28, 2011
Los Angeles Contemporary Exhibitions

FEATURING THE WORK OF:
Casey Alt
Zach Blas
Jeff Cain
Micha Cárdenas
Xárene Eskandar
Michael Kontopoulos
Elle Mehrmand
Christopher O'Leary
Claudia Salamanca
Pinar Yoldas

PERFORMANCE EVENT, June 30, featuring Zach Blas, Micha Cárdenas,
MAL IDEA, Elle Mehrmand, Christopher O'Leary, and Malcolm Smith.

PANEL DISCUSSION, July 28, featuring Jordan Crandall, Jack Halberstam,
and Rita Raley

EXHIBITION CATALOG DESIGN by Everett Pelayo
EDITED by Zach Blas & Christopher O'Leary

www.s-p-e-c-u-l-a-t-i-v-e.info

TABLE OF CONTENTS

Today, we see the world we live in as an inviable world, and yet a world poised for radical reconfiguration.

From global economic crises to pandemic panics to burgeoning forms of hatred and control to the ravaging of our earth, new borders and quarantines haunt and terrorize the world at stochastic levels of the global, nation-state, informatics, and the biological. Indeed, our world presents to us the seemingly complete commodification of life, culture, the body, the planet.

Yet, we find within these very inviabilities the kernels of potential to enact and push forward new ways, worlds, and lives.

In fact, we see many up-risings emerging everywhere: from the calls to action of militant groups like The Invisible Committee to the UC student protests to the insurrections of the Middle East to the digital activisims of WikiLeaks and Anonymous.

These all point toward living and existing in the world another way.

We see the SPECULATIVE as the uniting force in our artwork that conjures forth the potential of the world we want, in political, cultural, social, sexual, technological, biological, economic, and ecological dimensions.

The SPECULATIVE is that imaginative, aesthetic work done by the artist to create new possibilities, inspire change, gesture toward a livable future, and generate new tactics and methodologies.

The SPECULATIVE asks us to use our imagination politically.

The SPECULATIVE allows us to subvert reality; practice new types of activism; work with the impossible as a political framework; rediscover the magic of our materials; question what a body and collective is capable of; locate new sexualities and perversities; reconfigure capitalism, design, and branding; create new worlds, peoples, species, and ecologies; find embodiments and other productive actions that emerge from war, apocalypses, disasters, and death; and build our dream utopias.

—Zach Blas & Christopher O'Leary

Alexander R. Galloway

DOWN DISCOURSES

To see in a set formation--can a group of people do this? I was out in the city once, looking at the vast humanity all around me. Some collected in groups, but most were spread out in an unpredictable pattern, just as people do. But even then I could swear that they saw things in unison as a group. Of course there is no proof of this. Were they perhaps flocking together and seeing apart, or is there a communion of the eye, just as there is a communion of the body? A thought experiment: import all the laws of physics into vision. Gravity, inertia, and all the rest. And delete those same laws from all bodies. This is what happened that day in the city square.

I saw an assembly of bodies. No logic could catalog this sorry pile. It was as if the friction of the world had broken and changed, from a retardant into an accelerant. Anything that had served in former times to unify was now flooded with the most far flung extremes of behavior. No copies existed in the square. Each person was a singleton. No law unified them.

But for their eyes, law reigned supreme. For I sensed through some sort of premonition that all eyes were moving in unison. They moved back and forth together, as regular as the swinging of a pendulum. One would turn and immediately all others would follow. Having landed on a target, the weight of sight was felt by all. To reverse course required a special coordination of effort, just as a lumbering beast must slow and judge its balance carefully in order to change direction. The result was more a grand sweep than anything else. The power of it was impressive. I could see—by my solemn promise!—the rays of vision drawn across space as arrow-straight lines emanating from each skull. With all eyes moved together, the spotlight beams tended to form cones, with the points of each cone sweeping their illumination across the landscape.

These vision flocks produced a tremendous amount of heat. Just as a child might use a magnifying glass to set alight a dry leaf. Or just as Archimedes burned the ships.

HALF THE WORLD

Who is the first person and what are his most important qualities? I was told that the first person was seen trekking to the steps of a mighty house. Since this was high country, the house itself did not sit on a hill as most do, but was nestled in the beak of a soft depression between two proud hills. The first person approached and stopped, anxious. He had been here many times before. This house was his home.

Still he was anxious, for those who now live there had harassed him many times. There had been disputes over the crops. Someone had mismanaged the rotations. Some of the fallow fields had been put alight when they shouldn't have. So today the first person approached with caution. But when the door to the house opened, something strange occurred.

Across the threshold, the universe cleaved in half. All light that crossed from outside the threshold of the mansion bent back on itself, as if some grand mirror had been erected across the world to frame the bisection. When stepping over the sill, the directionality of the world reversed. What had exclusively shone in, now exclusively shone out. The inside of the house was existing solely to direct the outside, while the outside of the house was existing solely to be directed by the inside. The magnetism of the flows was absolute and ungovernable.

He is called the first person because he is captured as a seer. But he can never perform the capturing himself. It is the master-slave relation. Why? Because a victim is always shown face forward, but a tyrant is always shown from the back.

IS A FORM SMART OR NOT?

Consider the mighty oak of the hillside. One man says: Oh, the oak! You are a giant and your leaves cover a large area. It is you who were planted here, so many years before my birth. And after I am gone it shall be you still. At the end of each twig I see an acorn. These are your kin. For every kernel there may rise again a second oak, and a third! Can anything more beautiful exist? You move in a circle, a period. The small begets the large, all the while, and the large begets the small. You are selfsame, oh oak. This must be the key to life, that one grand form might somehow unloose a small piece of itself, a seed, so that the source might be duplicated again in miniature.

But next is another man: The oak! I have sat here under it each day of my life, but this day is absolutely new. You are raw, but not your touch, it is the curve of your branches that is raw, the extension of your trunk. I have never seen you before. Am I sick? Will I ever recover? Why is it that I see you day after day, year after year, but on each day you are different? Each different! If the sun is high in the sky, you have shade. If it snows, your leaves are gone. If a lumberjack should come, you would fall with a few quick swings of an ax. You offer me nothing. Your so-called love is really a form of negation. And so every day under you I withdraw and sleep.

A structure, once erected, stands tall. But rarely does one ask of it: Are you smart or are you not? It would be simple to respond in one clear way, that a form must be smart, for like a living organism, form endures. So wouldn't form itself represent a small shard of life? Just as a gene endures through many life cycles, so too does form. And so a form is truly the anti-fool, the cleverest of all.

But this is wrong. A form is not smart. A form is not smart--but not because it has no sense of itself. It is not smart because it has no sense of others. Form ignores. Only by standing in oblivion does one view structure.

SPRING

I wonder. I wonder why chickens and dogs, when they give birth, give birth to little chickens and dogs. The same, only much smaller. What a folly of biology. Would the cosmos not be more perfect if orangutangs spawned from eagles's nests, or a woman leaped from a rib? A soft fascism, this genetic kingdom, which obligates redundancy from its progeny. Am I trapped by this body? Am I not shackled all the more by this phylogeny? Each birth is a miracle. But no birth is a revelation. Why not blue babies from green mothers (or better, from fathers)? Why not slim stuffs from slime mold?

What came first, the chicken or the egg? Both, of course. Therein lies the problem. Hiding in the family tree of the chicken, no snake lurks in anticipation to swallow it up. The horseless carriage springs not from the horse. Only eggs and chickens all the way back.

The ancients knew about metamorphosis. But we moderns have lost all that. We have nothing but that most impoverished of concepts, change. We have no alchemy in our progeny. But for compensatory reward, flux rules supreme across the land of the living. Things evolve in perpetual motion, but never in metamorphosis. Springtime is no departure, only a return. The lust of the flesh intervenes only to shake the species backward toward a primordial constancy.

Fuck. Oh holy Spring! Ransack the houses and cupboards. Disencumber the sire of his possessions. Don't recognize the output of this profane megamachine. Find more holes please, and find them quickly. We desperately need evil children. Let them live and love and prosper and fight.

Alexander R. Galloway is an author and programmer. He recently ran a seminar at the Public School in Brooklyn, NY on "French Theory Today." He is currently writing a book on the aesthetics and politics of software.

particle group

TRANS_PATENT TALES: A PLAY FOR PARTICLES

Trans_patent 7,098,056, meta-materials and reverse friction containment.

Assingnee: Ulf Leonhardt and Thomas G Philbin, Casimir BioForce Inc.

Dates: Nov. 6, 2007 Expiration Jan 22,2089

ABSTRACT

Casimir nano-mirrors levitated a stream of particle 89 towards their new
host zones that the trans_patent agreements had set during the dipole
tensions a few seconds ago. It was a strong flow space to end up contracted
to—no neo-tribal force fields to enclose movement or shut down the ability
to circle so many para-attraction nodes. "Life is not so vital now, you have
to give a little to get a little." Ulf and Thomas were sitting naked around the
edges of the Surplus Vida bios as a velvet sun shivered in the distant horizon
of the Pacific through a large window. "I mean just look at us now." It was
true. The faces reflecting back at them were full of something more than life,
something more than desire, they were like new pearls born without friction.
The bioplugs clicked and de-linked. "Are you ready, baby?" After a brief
moment, a whisper came, "yes." Particle 89 started to unpack them into
quantum spins. It felt like love floating in an infinite mirror.

Quantum levitation by left-handed metamaterials http://www.iop.org/EJ/
abstract/1367-2630/9/8/254

[The stage is dark. Slow illumination of two white lab workers at
opposite ends of a long table and a large screen behind them, each sits
facing a computer.]

ACT ONE

Lab Worker One
Particle! Particle! Burning bright In the labs of the night,What posthuman
hand or eye could frame thy fearful trans_patenttry?

Lab Worker Two
In 2005 researchers in the University of Texas in the United States found that carbon nanotubes squirted into the trachea of mice caused inflammation of the lungs and granulomas (tumor-like nodules of bloated white blood cells in the lining of the lungs), and five of the nine mice treated with the higher dose died almost immediately.

Lab Worker One
In what gene deeps or skies Burnt the ownership of thine eyes? On what code dare it aspire? What IP dare seize the fire? And what patent, and what part, could twist the WIPO of thy heart? And when thy particles began to beat, What dread sensor? and what dread fleet?

Lab Worker Two
"Tiny Bits of Silver, Used As Bacteria-Eaters, Emerge As New Health Concern" (2011) *Science Survey* By Rae Tyson

Stinky socks may be socially embarrassing, but aren't in the same league as other pressing environmental issues. On the other hand, there may well be a connection between odor-resistant socks and an emerging health and environmental concern.

Scientists, environmentalists and regulators alike are increasingly concerned about nanosilver — microscopic particles that are now used for bacterial control in well over 1,000 consumer products. These include toys, cosmetics, sunscreen, air and water filters, household cleaners, clothing and washing machines. One increasingly common use of nanosilver is in athletic socks to minimize offensive smells. Though research is inconclusive, scientists have found evidence that nanosilver, once in the environment — most commonly in wastewater effluent — can potentially bioaccumulate in organisms such as earthworms, insects and fish. Studies also suggest that nanoparticles in soil can harm plants. http://www.sej.org/publications/sejournal/tiny-bits-silver-used-bacteria-eaters-emerge-new-health-concern

Lab Worker Two
What the atomic force hammer? what the chain? In what furnace was thy brain? What the chip? what circuit grasp dare its deadly errors clasp?

When the nanities threw down their gears, And watered ownership with their tears, Did K. Eric Drexler smile his work to see? Did nano-carbon 60 who made the Lamb make thee?

Lab Worker One
Trans_Patent 6608386: Sub-nanoscale electronic devices and bacterial processes

July 12, 2006 By Assignee(s) Yale University/YU (New Haven, CT) Inventors: Reed; Mark A. (Southport, CT); Tour; James M. (Columbia, SC)

Sometimes Lila would feel a bit itchy as she floated in her partner a few hours before integration. Most birthing was now a trans_patented condition involving sub-nanoscale trading – it was the only way to pay the cost of life now. So every hour during this last trimester Lila and her partner would ferment mass nanowire production on her in-vitro skin in collaboration with the YU bacteria colonies. She could feel the oldest most sustainable microbes on the planet staging WIPO-2 contracts for the latest off-scale metal-changing particles. Hundreds upon hundreds of YU products were waiting impatiently for her to catch a bit of crying air at the edges of her partner's canal to install and run – for just-in-time delivery. Delivery was all that mattered now.

Lab Worker Two
Nanoparticles in the lungs are translocated to the circulatory system and from there throughout the body, accumulating in the liver, spleen, and bone marrow. Nanoparticles inhaled through the nose and air passages are translocated to the brain through the olfactory nerves, and accumulate in the brain. Nanoparticles can enter the body through the skin; and quantum dots injected into the skin accumulate in lymph nodes with potential effects on the immune system.

ACT TWO

Lab Worker One
Particle Capitalism! Particle Capitalism! Burning bright in the labs of the night, What posthuman hand or eye Could frame thy fearful trans_patenttry?

Lab Worker One

"It is true that one cannot patent an element found in its natural form; however, if you create a purified form of it that has industrial uses – say, oxygen – you can certainly secure a patent." - Lila Feisee, Biotechnology Industry Organization's Director for Government Relations and Intellectual Property (2006).

Lab Worker Two

We are no longer under the sign of natural selection or even artificial selection —we are now under the force of particle selection. Everything on the planet, from indigenous aromas to public spaces to our atoms, is now forced to march into the World Intellectual Property Organization (WIPO) filters of globalization. The neo-liberal matrix that started to emerge fully in the 90's has played itself out on three stages: digital/Virtual Capitalism, genetic/Clone Capitalism and nanotechnology/Particle Capitalism. Each of these stages of techno-capital is being integrated via a new "deep harmonization" of the global Intellectual Property agenda: copyright laws, trademark laws and patent laws. A process that starts in the research chambers and ends in ownership enclosures, from patenting technology to patenting life, from patenting information to patenting atoms and creation of trans_patents.

Lab Worker Two

Trans_patent: 5,439,686

Assignee: Abraxis Bioscience, LA

Dates: Jan 7, 2005RX Expiration FEB 22,2083

ABSTRACT

"How small can anything be?" He asked her between infringements of her trans_patent by Abraxis Bio. Her left breast was now selling almost all paclitaxel* 10 particles as the matter market cycle hit a high value exchange. "How small can anything be?" He looked up at her and smiled. She kept the exchange open for any other pharma-particle bids. "We know creatures/ so tiny they would seem to disappear/If they were half their size." Her left breast was fading with each of the trespasses of her trans_patents – the cancer had been metastatic till now. He returned to his scan and recited: "How big do you suppose their livers are? Their hearts?/The pupils of their eyes?/Their toes?" The exchange was complete and recorded in Delware, Inc. She looked up at him with the slow gaze of the over-bought. "Pretty minute you must admit," he ended with a whisper. **

*http://www.drugpatentwatch.com/basic/preview/detail/index.php?search type=alpha&category=Generic&searchstring=PACLITAXEL **Lucretius, De Rerum Natura

Lab Worker One
Recombinant society falls quickly before nano-fest destiny. Biotechnology, like digital networks, becomes a side event before the next state of command and control society. Each of us will rapidly become the by-product of artificial nanotechnology "vitamins", interdependent molecular subassembly engines, and marked by inter-linked "termination dates." We will become more than replicants and less than nothing. The cross-roads between the imaginary and all too real construction of nanotechnology is perhaps already behind us.

Lab Worker Two
In the game of life and evolution there are three players at the table: human beings, nature, and machines. I am firmly on the side of nature. But nature, I suspect, is on the side of the machines.

Lab Worker One
Not much difference between a banana and a human. Same atoms, just arranged differently.

Lab Worker Two
Not much difference.

Lab Worker One
Not much difference at all.

[Both lab workers shut down their computers, eat a banana, and walk away.]

particle group is a collective consisting of Principal Investigators
Ricardo Dominguez (artivist), Diane Ludin (new media artist), Nina Waisman
(Interactive Sound Installation Design), and Amy Sara Carroll (poet/critic),
with a number of others flowing in and out. Assistant Researchers Marius
Schebella, Pierre Galaud, and Césaire José Carroll-Dominguez. The group
combines new media, the paraliterary, performance, artivism, and humor to
produce different gestures that forge a subversive relationship with the newest
frontiers of technological science in an effort to undermine some of their
assumptions of authority and power. *particle group* has exhibited at ISEA (San
Jose) 2006, House of World Culture (Berlin) 2007, "Inside the Wave" at the San
Diego Museum of Art 2008, Oi Futuro and FILE (Brazil) 2008, CAL NanoSystems
Institute (UCLA), 2009, Gallery atMedialab-Prado, Madrid (Spain), 2009, and
Nanosferica, (NYC) 2010.

pitmm.net

Jack Halberstam

GAGA MANIFESTO

(excerpt from a book in progress titled *Gaga Feminism,* forthcoming from The Feminist Press, 2012)

The manifesto, from Karl Marx to Valerie Solanas, has played with utopian possibility while also proposing a plan of action. For Karl Marx, the plan was for the workers of the world to rise up and take action against those who profit from their labor; for Valerie Solanas, the manifesto was a modest proposal, a contract with future generations of women whom she would save from the inequities of patriarchy by "cutting up men." For the Futurists, the manifesto voiced a break with the past, a definitive refusal to be bound to tradition and to be weighed down by history and expectation. And in Lady Gaga's new video, "Born This Way," the "Monster Mother's Manifesto" is some weird sci-fi shit about choosing good over evil after emerging from an egg covered in goo! Most manifestos combine the radical and the reactionary, the reasonable and preposterous, hard cold analysis with fantastical visions. I am using my Gaga Manifesto to push us further into the crisis, into the eye of the hurricane, deep into the heart of nonsense. And so...

In a crisis, in this crisis, don't remain calm... get agitated and add to the chaos.

"Organizations are obstacles to organizing ourselves."
        —*The Invisible Committee*

Welcome to the gagapocalypse! As the environmental crisis turns from bad to worse, as wars break out like wild fires across the globe, as bankers and corporate gamblers take higher and higher shares of the global markets and as the social rituals that formerly held communities together lose their meaning, it is time to go gaga. In a crisis, do not remain calm, do not look for the nearest exit, do not stick your head in the sand; do agitate, do make things worse, do run screaming through the street and do refuse to return to business as usual.

Business as usual is what created this mess in the first place. Business as usual has meant that business-men run/ruin the world and artists are out of luck; it has meant that education, spirituality, sexuality all must function on a business model and every attempt to make changes is greeted with a pragmatic question about whether changing things will also mean making money. Making money cannot be the goal of the new feminism. Putting women in positions of power is not what gaga feminism wants. What gaga feminism wants cannot be easily summarized but it is not an independent bank account, not a profitable non-profit; mama does not want a brand new bag. Mama wants revolution, but gaga revolution may not be one that Karl Marx or Valerie Solanas would recognize.

In Glenn Beck's favorite book to hate of the last few years, *The Coming Insurrection,* The Invisible Committee write on behalf of their manifesto: "Everyone agrees. It's about to explode." They go on to urge that we exploit the current economic crisis by blocking the economy; that we build upon the ruins of the social by reimagining relation within a "wild and massive experimentation with new arrangements and fidelities"; and that we "organize beyond and against work." The book, a kind of contemporary Situationist manifesto, is inspired in its logic and uncanny in its timing (given the recent insurrections around the globe from Europe to the Middle East) and it unites fragments from queer theory, "the future has no future," to punk DIY actions ("make the most of every crisis") and feminist insights about the implication of the family in the "great social debacle" that we called economic pros- perity ("everyone feels the inanity of the sad family nucleus"). The Invisible Committee also implicates university systems in the production of false hier- archies motored by people "who always ask permiss- ion before taking. Who silently respect culture, the rules, and those with the best grades. Even their attachment to their great critical intellectuals," they write, "and their rejection of capitalism are stamped by this love of school."

I love this little book, it speaks to me and about me, it calls me in a way that lots of the work that we do in the university does not. I like that it has no "author," that it refuses grand narratives and that it proceeds without the endless academic quarrels that drag down even the most inspired critical attempts to make bold interventions. The book engages some genres that we do not traffic in enough in as professors and as people who speak and write for a living – namely, manifestos, bold predictions, calls to arms—and it also names some important truths about failing economies, failing family structures, elitist universities and the opportunities that arise out of the ashes of an older form of politics as such. The book pulls together the strings of social upheaval and catches a slice of revolution in its net. "Everyone agrees," they write. "It's about to explode" – in Cairo, in Ramallah, in Athens, in Los Angeles, the insurrection is coming and the Invisible Committee urges us to "find each other" soon. It also reminds us that true anarchy is not the absence of all modes of organization, indeed effective anarchy requires that the ground be cleared first. But what creative anarchy does require is that we organize separate from organizations, because "organizations are an obstacle to organizing ourselves."

In *Fragments of An Anarchist Anthropology*, speculative intellectual David Graeber provides plenty of examples of societies that live and have lived without state forms or capitalist economies. While many of these societies are quickly dismissed by skeptics as "primitive," Graeber proposes that the division between primitive and modern has been overstated and that even though there are important distinctions between contemporary culture grounded in technology and impersonal communication and pre-modern societies invested in contact and cooperation, there are also many lines of continuity that we can trace in order to find traces of anarchist possibilities. Arguing for more imaginative leaps, less skepticism, and "blowing up walls," Graeber, like other speculative and utopian intellectuals, finds evidence of alternative political imaginaries everywhere he looks. "Why," he asks "are there so few anarchists in the academy?" The obvious answer is that academy precisely trains smart people to think in 'disciplined' ways, to think, in other words, in ways that are inherently antithetical to anarchy.

On behalf of more anarchy, less state, cooperative social forms and brand new sex/gender systems, I offer up Gaga Feminism – a form of feminism that advocates going gaga, being gaga, running amok, physically and intellectually, and in the process finding new languages with which to imagine, craft and implement a different way of living, loving and making art.

Jack Halberstam, a professor at USC, just finished a book for Duke University Press titled *The Queer Art of Failure* (forthcoming, 2011). Halberstam is the author of three other books, including *Female Masculinity* (1998), and tries to be an inorganic, renegade, public intellectual. When that does not work, Halberstam is known for making lots of trouble, being abrasive and refusing to compromise. While working on these personality flaws or advantages, depending upon your perspective, Halberstam is also writing a book to be published in 2012 by The Feminist Press titled *Gaga Feminism*. It might change the way we think about sex and gender, it might not. I hope it does.

Sean Dockray

FURTHER NOTES ON AN ESCAPE ACT

On the occasion of the invitation to contribute some writing
to the exhibition catalogue for *Speculative,* I figured that
I would use the opportunity to expand on a particular ongoing
project. My interest in doing so is to ask about how we might
deploy this notion of the speculative in relation to *this* immed-
iate context – the art exhibition and the social practice of art,
more generally.

David Graeber, when thinking about why there are relatively
many communists teaching at Universities compared to anarchists, suggests that the University is perfectly compatible with
external analysis and theorizing, whereas ethical transforma-
tions of practice and organization are practically off limits. The
slow heaviness of institutions, pronounced inequalities of
power, and silent political maneuverings all resist this kind of
change. The mechanisms of exclusion in the field of art are
a little bit different. Rather than actively policing boundaries
(you can't be seen because you're not there) art operates on the
regime of visibility (you can't be seen because you can't be seen;
you are not legible). There is certainly a growing overlap between these two systems, such as MFA and PhD programs,
teaching jobs, residencies, project grants, which supplement
the more obvious gatekeeping (museums, critics, curators,
commissaires d'exhibition).

All of this is not to say that there isn't a lot of change in the
various positions that one might take in the field of art: curator,
critic, artist, writer, collector, gallerist, publisher, promoter,
and so on. Over the decades, the possibilities available to an
individual in any one of these positions has changed, imbuing
some with more power at certain historical moments. More than
that, one could argue that in addition to an innovative body
of work, cultural producers can distinguish themselves through
an innovative performance of some combination of these roles.
The implication, of course, is that artists have been among the
avant-garde of neoliberal labor forms. From competitive self-

entrepreneurship to flexible working requirements to confusing leisure and labor, to the precarity that all of this inevitably leads to, artists experience these conditions quite generally now.

None of this can be divorced from the financialization of just about everything, including art. Not only is art bought and sold, but the work of cultural workers generates increased real estate values, provides added value to otherwise unremarkable products, encourages investment, and so on. We have speculative entities like the Artist Pension Trust that redirect tendencies of mutual support and social responsibility towards faith in the market (while at the same time, trying to game the system). Regardless of some of the very admirable motivations of the company, APT imagines a collection of artists as a mutual fund, relying on exclusion to generate value. Obviously, it is a symptom of the last decade, and in the language of the internet, a meta-producer or aggregator rather than a new collectivity.

Speculation is a normative condition for artists. Who can possibly plan? Institutions are fickle, unstable, and interdependent. Most activity is necessarily contingent, our time is given to what opportunities exist, to what money we need to pay for the essentials, to what might make more opportunities. It would seem then, that speculation is a potential site of contestation, or to put it another way, that some speculative cultural work ought to be directed towards "building a new world in the shell of the old world," as the Industrial Workers of the World might put it.

This is not a new call. If anything, it is simply an attempt to add my voice into a building, collective call. A few scattered examples, close to home, that spring to mind immediately are the Eternal Telethon, the computer programming language Processing, Upload Download Perform, the Elysian Park Museum of Art, and The Public School. But rather than provide a survey of what already exists, I wanted to conclude by expanding on a proposal that I've made a couple of times over the past year, in Aarhus and Cairo.

The proposal is for an escape act, and I want to admit from the beginning that I don't think I could follow through with it myself, which is perhaps the reason I want to keep returning to it. It begins with the question: rather than taking authorship as a monolithic axiom of contemporary capitalism to be affirmed or opposed (and the possibility, let alone the efficacy, of opposition is a question here), perhaps we can think of it as a mechanism, or a process, or a point of intervention?

The proposal is for the formation of something that is in between a school, a collective, a secret society, and a union. A group of artists agree to the following five rules:

First, we lose our real names. This is not an absolute change of identity, but rather, we will count our number and then invent that many fictional individuals.

Second, all of our cultural activity, whether individual or aggregate, will be done under one or more of these fictional names. It is not simply that each of us will have an alter ego, but that we all have a multiplicity of alter egos available to use.

Third, when one of these characters is invited to an exhibition, residency, lecture, interview, performance, teaching position, or whatever, then any of us, and any number of us, might go. It will be a matter of collective discussion or convenience.

Fourth, when any money is earned through sales, salary, commission, or stipend, it is shared equally.

Fifth, if one of us wants to exit this arrangement, then we will "kill" one of the fictional individuals. The specifics of that are up to those who remain.

That's it. Naturally, it's the first point that is the most difficult to come to follow through with; it's the inverted mirror image of the death in the fifth point. The obvious question becomes, what it is that we do with all of our past work? The kultural kapital in the room looms very large. Perhaps some works, maybe even degrees, can be reassigned, but not all. And the related question, what to do with our social networks? Perhaps it will turn out that half of our social networks will be sympathetic to the escape act and play along, while the other half really won't care because it makes no difference to them whether they have befriended an image or not.

If all is going well, the act turns from a redistribution of works and networks to a communization of skills and abilities. In Cairo, the group of us knew a total of 7 languages fluently, which we decided would be an important component of the cast of characters that we would develop. For example, we invented a computer programmer who also made translations (presumably of fiction and theory).

This is not to say that the characters need to be stable. In the same way that I might produce a piece of writing as The Writer and then a painting as The Painter, it might be that The Painter writes some poetry and then a letter to the editor and then starts a weblog. Six people might be involved in all of those things. The tensions between promiscuity and discipline, individuality and collectivity, are there to play with and not a source of irreconcilable anxiety.

Perhaps the most obvious thing about the proposal is that it doesn't exactly escape the market but tries to weasel its way into a new relationship with the market. For example, in order to resist commodification, one might choose to produce work that is immaterial, temporary, or even collectively authored. But time has demonstrated that the art market is quite capable of integrating the unsellable, provided someone sees value in it. The escape act may very well produce objects that are more market-ready than any of the individuals might produce on their own. I'm not sure if this is a problem with the proposal or not, but it is certainly something that gets worked out internally among the group. Maybe they are subsidizing the rest of their practices. Maybe they secretly long to make easily consumable things.

It's said that the hardest time for collectives is when they have success, and it is certainly unknown how the escape act would internally respond to success, although it is written into the bylaws. Maybe someone will want to go solo? Maybe someone will become saddled with the responsibility of being the "value producer" and will grow to resent that.

And when these characters are fictional to begin with, what obligation does the group have to be faithful to them? Are their stories written or improvised? Might their names change over time? According to what system or scale could such questions be answered? Potential income? Overall narrative? Ethics? Art History?

The more I think about it, the more I come to think that an escape act probably is quite limited in its transformative potential. Maybe a group of people could pull it off, but what would that amount to, beyond those people? I suppose there could be many such groups, but would that just become some kind of Balkanized cultural theater? Or would such an exodus, in the spirit of Paolo Virno, modify the conditions under which relations of domination and financialization have managed to prosper?

Sean Dockray lives in Los Angeles. He is an artist and a founding director of Telic Arts Exchange, a non-profit arts organization providing a critical engagement with new media and culture. Dockray initiated The Public School and AAAARG.ORG and last summer he co- organized an itinerant seminar in Berlin, "There is nothing less passive than the act of fleeing," in collaboration with Caleb Waldorf and Fiona Whitton. They are continuing their work together as The Public School later this year in the Encuentro Internacional de Medellín 2011. He has recently participated in "Speak, memory" at the Townhouse Gallery in Cairo, the Second World Congress of Free Artists in Aarhus, a commission for the 2010 New York Art Book fair, the 29th São Paulo Biennial, Properties of the Autonomous Archive in Bombay, the exhibition, "Shadowboxing," at the Royal College of Art in London, and is a co-chair of the Mobility Shifts conference in New York. Dockray's writing has been published in *Cabinet*, *Bidoun*, *X-TRA*, *Volume*, and *Fillip*.

Pedro Lasch

BRAIN REVIEW 2002

(PART 1)

http://www.design.ru/posters/brain/
brain-800x600.jpg

Published as e-mail with links to
images in March 2002 through temporary
address thekeypboardisdead
@yahoo.com

Note: The author does not claim ownership
of the images used to illustrate this piece,
only of their linking within the narrative.
The life span of each link varies like the
neurons in our brain. All of the links in-
cluded were active at time of publication.
Like dead neurons, many of them will not
be with us at a later period.

START

http://www.canoe.ca/OutpostWWWIm-
ages/brain.gif

When you walk into the exhibition, you
see a line of home appliances flanking
every inch of wallspace. The size and
character of the gallery is, ideally, like the
kitchen from *The Shining*. There are

washing machines, toasters, stoves, refrigerators, microwave ovens, shaving machines, lamps, computers, monitors, telephones, fax machines. There are photo-copiers, video-cameras, exercise machines, radios, sound systems, alarm-clocks, fire detectors, hair-driers, electric drills, one or two vibrators and a fan on the ceiling. There is water, heating and air-conditioning. It is a studio, home and office, anything but a factory.

Except for all these appliances covering the walls, the floor is completely empty. It could be wood, tile or concrete. In the center of the room there is an empty fishtank — standing on a pedestal about 4 feet high. On the upper right-hand corner of the tank a little card gives the viewer some necessary information.

"Please touch the brain. The brain is made of a hyper-sensitive texture and contains a complex network of remote control switches, which operate all the appliances present in this room."

http://www.csm.ornl.gov/SC99/brain.jpg

When one looks down at the floor, one discovers small pools and traces of water. When I went to the gallery, an old man was playing the brain as if he was a kid. He had obviously experimented with it for a while, since by now he had a fair amount of control of the room's lighting, and was able to play with the volume of the music and the noises and melodies produced by the various appliances.

http://www.lanl.gov/orgs/pa/News/brain.jpeg

http://www.nlm.nih.gov/pubs/nlmnews/pictures/brain.gif

But what seemed to be the major attraction in coming to this show was observing the uncanny similarity of this brain with those the visitors had seen in museums of natural history and anatomy books. Most of them would not touch the brain on their first visit. It was too real, too wet, and it looked too mushy.

Once returning, they would hold it like a baby, drop it, or throw it away with a combination of disgust and hatred. One girl banged it against the wall until it split in half, showing the myriads of cables and transistors.

So far, the artist has brought in more than ten brains due to extreme handling by the audience.

http://www.studentbmj.com/back_ issues/0901/life/brain%20pizza.JPG

The curiosities abound. Someone put the brain in the washing machine, causing all the appliances to shriek and turn in a bizarre, unpredictable, spherical pattern until the gallerist was forced to intervene in the insane performance. Someone else tried to bite away a chunk of it. One thing is sure: it was always fascinating to watch people play the brain.

From freakish novelty to intimate contact, the brain became an everyday experience. The artist sold many expensive copies to museums and private households. The brain was now fun and easy to use.

People started having conversations about the particularities and character of their new domestic companion. Brains were seen flying out of windows or kicked around like a ball by prankish kids in department stores.

http://www.adirondackballoonfest.org/brain.jpg

Pirate brains appeared in the markets of every major Third World city. The U.S. military and its associated universities began designing a version that could be hooked up directly to its model, thus eliminating the limitations of the sense of touch.

http://www.umich.edu/~trekclub/Pictures/brain.GIF

Few cared to ask what the brains were made of, or where they were produced.

http://www.newgrounds.com/cat/images/brain.gif

END

Pedro Lasch was born and raised in Mexico City. Since 1994, he divides his time between Durham (NC), where he teaches art, art theory, and visual studies at Duke University, and New York (NY), where he leads on-going projects with immigrant communities and art collectives, such as 16 Beaver Group.

His solo exhibitions include *Open Routines/Rutinas Abiertas* (Queens Museum of Art, 2006) and *Black Mirror/Espejo Negro* (Nasher Museum of Art, 2008); his projects have also been presented at Baltimore Museum of Art, Walker Art Center, MASS MoCA (U.S.A.), Baltic: The Centre for Contemporary Art, Royal College of Art (U.K.), Museo de Arte Reina Sofía (Spain), Centro Nacional de las Artes (Mexico), The Singapore Art Museum (Singapore), the Gwangju Biennial (South Korea), as well as the AND AND AND platform of Documenta 13 (Germany). A selection of his works can be found at:

http://www.pedrolasch.com/

Scott Bukatman

Some years ago I lifted a phrase from William Burroughs — hey, everybody else was doing it. "Your entire planet is being developed into terminal identity and complete surrender" he wrote, and I saw that phrase as articulating two positions with regard to the contemporary subject — the end of identity, and a new identity fomented at the computer screen or terminal. The world was going digital. Computers, once room-sized behemoths crunching numbers for governments, scientists, and corporations, had entered the home — to do what, many of us weren't quite sure. But there they were, with their cathode ray screens and CPUs. It was a strange technology, strange in its non-visibility. A technology with no moving parts (other than that floppy disk drive) but which moved data around the world at unprecedented speeds. Television began to wane as be the emblem of liveness in the world of media. *TRON* and *Neuromancer* appeared, both fed by the same desire — the desire to understand what was happening behind those screens, to know how the movement of hand-on-mouse translated into actions in another realm. Both works gave us bodies, the better to know our disembodiment. Well, that's actually too arch and could be phrased otherwise. The better to resist our disembodiment, might be another may of parsing their programs. The better to begin to know the new world by translating into the terms of embodiment by which we knew our regular world, is still another, and the one I pushed the hardest in *Terminal Identity*.

Now I show my students *TRON* and ask, "Why was *TRON*?" Why did we need it? What problem or question was it addressing? They *have* no idea. That the world behind the screen might need to be under-stood was an alien concept. To begin with, our screens now *have* no "behinds." The laptop screen has nothing behind it, ditto the glassy surfaces of smartphones and iPads. They are all surface, the "behind" now entirely metaphorical, and, further, a metaphor that has out-lived its usefulness. What mattered was whether or not the technology worked, not *how* it worked. Really, who still cared?

But when technology becomes so comfortable, it becomes effectively invisible and seemingly natural. What is natural need not be questioned, only given. And so, with our new tools and toys, it's enough to be able to Skype, Tweet, shop, and play Angry Birds. Why not? But as the curators of SPECULATIVE point out, our global village has become a village of the damned: a place of panic, pandemics, punditry, and powerlessness; our political systems, bodies, and environments ravaged; the alternates to the full commodification of existence now inconceivable. If I envisioned terminal identity as, at least in part, a configuration of awareness that might help us avoid that state of "complete surrender," well, it seems that the opposite has come to pass, and complete surrender is all we can offer.

The curators and artists and scholars, and curator-artist-scholars, of **SPECULATIVE** want to make it all strange again. They propose new technologies that articulate the crisis, ready to shock, annoy, ironize, and in general to serve as a positive nuisance. They want to worry us, to turn the tables on our programming. These are artifacts from a future museum that maps our decline and fall. And if I don't fully embrace their spirit of crisis that undergirds their show, I endorse the spirit of intervention and their desire to use technology that moves beyond the utopian emptiness of "social" media. This is anti-social media, and it's what we need now.

Scott Bukatman is an Associate Professor in the Film and Media Studies Program at Stanford University and is the author of *Terminal Identity: The Virtual Subject in Postmodern Science Fiction*, and *Matters of Gravity: Special Effects and Supermen in the 20th Century*. His latest is the forthcoming *The Poetics of Slumberland: Animated Spirits and the Animating Spirit*.

Jordan Crandall

INTO THE ALLEYWAY

I am standing amid a city street teeming with actors,
awash in rhythms and sensations, sounds and lights.
The street courses with electricity and computational force,
　　　transmissions of energy, information, materials, and goods.

People, parts, event-components, and atmospheric elements.
Sounds, smells, measurements.
Ideas, compositions, settings.
Vehicles, vibrations, words.

Restless, agitated actors negotiate their way through urban pathways, leaving their traces on
the city's interfaces, objects, and systems. They maneuver for attention, intimacy, and
relevance, banding and disbanding, accumulating and releasing, extending and
consolidating. They are concentrated and networked, transcendent and cumulative,
immanent and originless.
Composed through linguistic, sensory, and rhythmic exchanges,
they are excessive,
impersonal,
of indeterminate form,
rendered public and precarious,
not at the center,
not primary or alone.

They receive and return movement. They update and extend. They choose, yet offer
themselves to choice. They act, yet are acted upon. They ready themselves to maneuver in
this actionability. They cultivate their sustained modulation in the gatherings through which
they move, and as they do so, they negotiate adherence to the demands for movement and
attendance that these gatherings make. They acclimate to the prevailing terms of their
structural inclination, which condition apprehension in time.

The inclinations of the street are embodied in its sensations, rhythms, forces.
Its atmospheric heat, smell of vehicle exhaust, rumblings of pedestrians, textures of dirt and
sweat.
Its travel patterns, timetables, transfer hubs, interchanges, regulations, routes, habits.
Its constellations of signals, signs, social expectations, and productivity demands.
Pulsating with attractive energies,
　　　they harness my attention, my desire.
They pull me forward, compelling me to *move on*.
I surrender to the pressure to *do* — to link up, to transfer weight over land, to move in
accordance with the norm.
I acquiesce to the need to endure *as* something, something coded and felt, in concert with
the actors that offer themselves for attachment, transfer, and conduction. The gatherings
that offer consistency and meaning.

To linger involves risk.
When movement runs counter to the norm of a given place or *pace*, an EVENT is conjured.
I do not want to deviate from the norm to this degree: I do not want, myself, to become
EVENT. Rather, I want to merge into one: an event beyond myself, to whose standards I
can cede.

I want to adhere to its conditions, its cooperative demands.
I want to absorb myself in its galvanizing force.
I want to channel its excessiveness, *expose* myself to it.
I want to bathe in the flows of its norm.

And yet:
while the EVENT is an exceptional occurrence, a deviation,
it is also a cooperative gathering, an affirmation.
It is situated in the midst of the fugitive and the common.
A coherence destabilized and amplified,
congealing in tandem with the normalization of a surround.

While I aim to avoid detection, I also seek to cultivate it:
          to offer myself for selection, conduction, and bonding.
I am diffused yet distinctive, concealed yet appearing.
I move between the solicitor, selectable and exceptional, and the hidden, invisible and
utterly ordinary.
I am conditioned by the primacy of display.
However configurative or fleeting my presence; however singular, multiple, or scalar my
agency,
I position myself as a potential EVENT.
In my movement, coding, and manner, I signal my availability for affiliation.

+
In the darkness a man lingers.
Aficionado of renegade gatherings, he dwells amid the ebb and flow of movement,
          in the midst of the fugitive and the infinite.
He seeks a generative danger, a potent mixture of desire and threat.
He is far from the leisurely or productive dweller of the street.
He lingers in its renegade zones, unlit, unmapped, and unnamed.
Passageways for services, shortcuts, discreet comings and goings.
Interstitial, discarded spaces, unaffected by commodification and spectacle.
Shadowy recesses, strewn with ad-hoc features and ugly facades.
Receptacles rife with smells.

He browses, yet he seeks that which is not fully compatible with the world of consumerism and thought.

Up ahead: a potential consort. He stops, loiters at the corner, leans back against a wall. Ambiguous glances signal both availability and withdraw; dark folds of clothing both expose the body and cloak it. A combinatory stance, hips forward but head turned away. Actions framed, assembled, and cued. A behavioral composite into which movement and intention are inferred. The qualified sense of arousal: is his desire aimed at me; in what way; to what degree? *What does he want of me?* What is the nature of my own desirability? In response, the man checks himself. Mirror, gauge, valve. Reflect, calibrate, modulate. Smooth the hair, straighten the clothes, adjust the body. In response to an imagined query, which envelops him like moisture in the air, he defines his contours.

Yet there are no counterparts to this desire, only internal parts of its architecture, opaque to observation.
Actors are gathered and constituted within its immanent, extensive circuits of transmission.

The alleyway architecture helps to organize a rhythm of interaction: a gathering and flow.
The standardized speeds of the urban terrain — of the streets running alongside — do not necessarily apply.
Territory is creatively inhabited, rewritten, reprogrammed.
Time is reformatted and regained.
Movements are characterized by disruption and distraction: they unfold at different rhythms, in various directions and dimensions.
The possibility of encounters, the readability of glances and gestures, are magnified — however they are reciprocated or avoided.
Contact of another sort is cultivated: transient, random events, unexpected and strange.
The EVENT that should not be sought; the EVENT that one should not endeavor to *become.*
The cultivation of anomalous behavior as event rather than its prevention
          -- or its detection, tracking, and classification.

The event becomes a generative mechanism:
          a practice involving the reorientation, production, and expansion of occurrences.
A transformation of the ordinary incident by way of a destabilization of the familiar.

An external agency is met without preconceptions,
unfiltered through a scaffold of preferences, categories, and standards.
Contact is made with a stranger, an actor that is not *known.*
Epistemological constraints are exceeded,
ontological investment amplified.

The event provides an opening, a gateway into another relational condition.
Its cultivation requires patience, sensitive awareness, attunement to that which congeals in the here-and-now:
an avoidance of emphasis on the "what comes next" in favor of the extended, absorptive field of the already-there.
A resistance to the terms of inclination.
A readiness devoid of expectation.
An attunement to the priorities of a shared situation:
how the event *matters* in the embodied stances and positions of its attending actors,
        as it is sustained in practice.

The "source" of action is in the situation. The situation calls the action out of its attending actors; the action flows through them. Actors cooperatively negotiate with the materials of an event, receiving knowledge from the circumstances, cultivating the skill for discerning the meanings that are embodied there. They attune to what the situation calls for, what it reveals as appropriate or opportune.

An ethics of the event,
occupied not with selfhood but with a dynamic field of actors,
        copresent and cooperatively maneuvering.

+

Amid this alleyway teeming with actors, traversed by rhythms, sensations, and vibrations, the lingering man, a divergence-assembly amidst the flows, has become an object of analysis,
        positioned within a rhetorical and observational domain.
He has also become a figure:
a complex of actualized practices,
an embodiment of observation, attunement, and narration routines,
an agent that invites our identification and affiliation.
Depending on the expectations that accompany the various domains through which this renegade figure is seen, we may be frustrated or intrigued. The solicitations may be heeded or resisted. Positions occupied or denied.

To linger involves risk.

In the twisting and turnings, in the forward movements and the retreats, the agent wanders, disperses and consolidates.
With a contingent ontological status,
it floats in and out of the scene, dwelling with and upon the phenomena that is registered,
        enacting an absorptive relinquishment that undermines a platform of mastery.
Readily diffused within the gatherings and flows of bodies, it moves within, and engenders, a type of situation that resists consolidation in terms of identity.

The passage between authority and relinquishment, distant protection and immersive imperilment, opens a destabilized zone.

Reckless phenomena surges forth, full of abandon and disorder, violence, asssembly, and decomposition.

A potential zone of contact to "otherness" is orchestrated, without having a personalized object of desire in mind.

An *excessive proximity*, so close that it resists personality and conceptualization, opens at the level of agency, time, and space, intertwined with urban configurations that it both responds to and structures:

> an EVENT beyond self, to whose standards one can cede.

Unconventional relational forms come into play,

> extensive and conductive,
>
> > involving the promiscuous cultivation of similarity and accordance.

Transmission, attunement, calibration.
Correspondence, redundancy, standardization.

Dynamically stabilized forms of copresence

> configure and fluctuate
>
> in degrees of resemblance and constraint.

Logics of self-enclosure are reorganized. Oppositional differences cede to solicitous accordances:

> extensions within an ontology of correspondence,
>
> > a teeming, vibratory instantaneity of immanent, configurable likeness.

Possessive bases of knowledge-accumulation are relinquished.
Agency is multiplied, not diminished,
constituted not in reduction but in dissemination:
not where it is *not*, but where it already *is*.
It does not aim to recuperate an incomplete interiority, but to modulate an amplified externality:

> a matter of directing energy or desire rather than restricting it.

This is an extensive, "resolute openness" — as when I say I "resolve to love."
An implicated, absorptive, receptive attending, divested of claims

> — a zone of intimacy devoid of capture.

My desire is not to possess an object, in such a way as it would fulfill a fundamental lack.
Rather, this extension, rife with excess energy and potential, activates the abundance already within me: it shows me what I already have.

Jordan Crandall is an artist, theorist, and performer based in Los Angeles. He is Associate Professor in the Visual Arts Department at University of California, San Diego. His video installations, presented in numerous exhibitions worldwide, combine formats and genres deriving from traditional cinema as well as military and surveillance culture, exploring new regimes of power and their effects on subjectivity, sociality, embodiment, and desire. His most recent video, *HOTEL* (2010), produced in advanced, 4K high definition technology, probes into the realms of extreme intimacy, where techniques of control combine with techniques of the self. He is the 2011 winner of the Vilem Flusser Theory Award, given by the Transmediale and the Vilem Flusser Archive in Berlin. He is also the founding editor of the new journal *VERSION*. He is currently developing a new book and performance project called *GATHERINGS* -- a performative study of the nature of the event and the new forms of awareness, cognition, and material agency that are emerging in data-intensive environments.

Casey Alt

BEING DERIVATIVE: THE FUTURE OF SPECULATIVE PRACTICE

A VACILLOGIX™ WHITE PAPER

"For the merchant, even honesty is a financial speculation." [1]
    — Charles Baudelaire

"Business art is the step that comes after Art." [2] — Andy Warhol

"The future is already here — it's just not evenly distributed." [3]
    — William Gibson

In considering the value of speculative operations in artistic practice, we at VacilLogix™ believe that such analyses must be grounded in the comparative. Particularly when considered in relation to the significantly more robust discipline of financial speculation, artistic speculative practice appears impoverished at best. This assessment begs the glaring question: Why have financial speculative practices advanced so rapidly whereas speculative arts practices have not?

While one might object to such a comparison on grounds of incommensurability between the two fields, artistic speculation and financial speculation are highly congruent practices. As originally demonstrated by sociologist Pierre Bourdieu, any robust social analysis must consider not only financial capital but also the equally important forms of social capital and cultural capital, with all three categories being mutually convertible. [4] The last of these, cultural capital or *cool*, is the primary jurisdiction of the arts. Given Bourdieu's law of conservation of capital within a social system, new forms of financial or cultural capital can only be created at the expense of others. Within the past few decades, the most lucrative and prolific conversions have been the liquidation of social capital into either financial or cultural capital — a process we call *sociopathic abstraction*. In this way, financial and artistic speculation share fundamentally similar mechanisms.

It is no accident that the phrase *speculative practice* has become virtually synonymous with financial speculation. Financial speculation has become so advanced a profession and so formidable a social force as to remake its parent science of economics from within. Early economists were careful to distinguish between the terms *investment* and *speculation*, with original differences

---

1. Charles Baudelaire, "My Heart Laid Bare," sct. 97, *Intimate Journals* (1887), trans. by Christopher Isherwood.

2. Andy Warhol, *The Philosophy of Andy Warhol* (Orlando: Harvest Books, 1975), 92

3. William Gibson, quoted in *The Economist*, December 4, 2003.

4. Pierre Bourdieu, "Ökonomisches Kapital, kulturelles Kapital, soziales Kapital," in *Soziale Ungleichheiten* (Soziale Welt, Sonderheft 2), ed. Reinhard Kreckel (Goettingen: Otto Schartz & Co., 1983), 183-198.

hinging on assessment of risk. While investment promised a safe and satis-factory return on financial commitment, speculation was considered much riskier with no guarantees on either principal or return.[5] The fact that the term *speculation* has all but fallen out of usage might suggest that financial speculation has itself disappeared. Yet the truth is precisely the opposite: financial activities have become so overwhelmingly speculative as to render previous distinctions meaningless. The irony is that nearly everything we currently regard as the more historically palatable practice of "investment" is actually speculation.

Such wholesale usurpation of the economic landscape testifies to the immense potency of contemporary speculative financial practices. While one might postulate several reasons for this flourishing, our research overwhelmingly indicates that this success flows from a single factor: the comprehensive yoking of speculative practice to algorithmic comp-utation of sociopathic abstractions.

In both technical and common parlance, abstraction is often defined as creating a representational surrogate for an actual object or relationship. At the most basic level, all financial objects are abstractions of a creditor-debtor relationship between two or more social entities. The modern conven-tion of standardized monetary systems is perhaps the most indispensible sociopathic abstraction. Its value derives from transmuting the social imme-diacy of the creditor-debtor relationship into a depersonalized system of discretely calculable quantities of fungible value. More importantly, this foundational layer of abstraction facilitates extrapolation to higher levels (abstractions from abstractions) called *derivatives*, which have become the bread and butter of contemporary speculative financial practice.

The art of abstraction-based financial speculation took a dramatic leap forward in 1973 when Fischer Black and Myron Scholes published their partial differential equation that enabled accurate calculation of the price of financial derivatives based on the values of underlying assets.[6] The Black-Scholes model sparked frenzied expansion of the financial derivatives market, fueled in part by a parallel acceleration in the digital computer technologies required to per-form the intensive Black-Scholes calculations. During the ensuing decades,

---

5. For a more extensive discussion of early economic distinctions between investment and speculation, see Benjamin Graham and David's *Security Analysis* (McGraw-Hill Book Company, 1934).

6. Fischer Black and Myron Scholes, "The Pricing of Options and Corporate Liabilities," *Journal of Political Economy* 81/3 (1973): 637–654.

the capacity for so-called "algo-trading" of financial derivatives has matured at (literally) lightning pace into the highly abstracted, real-time, globalized financial network that exists today, with algo-trades currently comprising over 80% of all trades across major financial markets.

While critics such as John Lanchester have convincingly argued that post-structural practices of the 1960s and 70s afforded comparable opportunities for sociopathic abstraction in the arts, little has come of them.[7] Though innovations such as the Nielsen ratings system have made some inroads towards abstractly quantifying cool, their inherently closed methodologies have only served to further consolidate cultural capital within a shrinking cabal of mass media corporations. As a result, one can attribute much of the historical gap in progress between financial and artistic speculative practice to artistic speculation's lack of an open and robust methodology for sociopathic abstraction as well as the digital software for calculating such derivatives.

Fortunately, this dire diagnosis is rapidly proving outdated. Social media applications such as Facebook, YouTube, and Twitter have made remarkable strides in creating global computational platforms for abstracting human social relations into cleanly computable units of cool. Mechanisms such was Facebook's "Like" tally, Twitter follower numbers, or YouTube view counts have become the standardized currencies of cultural capital. Accordingly, the social media sites themselves have evolved into sophisticated trading exchanges whose daily transaction volumes rival those of major financial markets. As a comparison, the New York Stock Exchange boasts a current daily trade volume of 1.6 billion shares, whereas YouTube claims over 2 billion video views each day. Facebook averages over 23 billion minutes of daily usage with over a billion pieces of content shared daily amongst its roughly 500 million members.[8]

This rapid drive towards digitization of all social transactions has also prompted convergence between financial and cultural practices. Savvy financial speculators have designed new algo-trading systems that intuitively sample social media traffic to anticipate changes in consumer sentiment.[9] Further, financial exchanges themselves increasingly mimic social media

7. John Lanchester, "Melting into Air," *New Yorker*, November 10, 2008, 82-3.

8. NYSE, NYSE Statistics Archive, http://www.nyse.com/financials/1022221393023.html; YouTube, Statistics, http://www.youtube.com/t/press_statistics; Facebook, Press Room, Statistics, http://www.facebook.com/press/info.php?statistics.

9. Nick Gentle, "'It's Like the Matrix:' Twitter May Help Read Investors' Minds," *Bloomberg News* (October 21, 2010); Graham Bowley, "Computers That Trade on the News," *The New York Times* (December 22, 2010).

startup ventures, as new generations of highly automated and exclusive "dark pool" exchanges suck financial liquidity away from traditional public exchanges.[10] Additionally, both sides have been beset by fears regarding the very algorithmic speed that has prompted their proliferation. Within the financial realm, critics allege that the widespread adoption of automated high-frequency trading software has contributed to increased volatility of financial markets, as evidenced by the unsettling "Flash Crash" of May 2010 in which high-frequency algo-trading software triggered a 9% drop in the Dow Jones Industrial Average within a matter of minutes.[11] Similarly, recent neuroscience research has condemned the "rapid-fire" nature of social media, arguing that the technologies undercut the temporal threshold required for human moral evaluative processes, particularly among young adults.[12] Nevertheless, the headlong integration of the two fields continues unabated, and recent oppositions seem to have only hastened their fusion.

This inexorable folding of financial and artistic speculation into a unified field of digital operations heralds unprecedented opportunities for generating novel forms of speculative practice. It signals the birth of entirely new breeds of sociopathic value derivatives in which speculative dealings with presiding social mores are as easy as buying and selling commodities futures. Imagine the value proposition inherent in short-selling patriotism, hedging against authenticity, or optioning inequality. This new generation of social value derivatives, specifically designed to sidestep prevailing social controls, holds the promise of complete liquidation of historically frozen hoards of social capital into a fluid, free-flowing field of timely, adaptive, uncertain, and utterly anarchic capital.

Fortunately, this transformation will not be up for debate and is already underway. The ingenious thing about sociopathic derivatives is their ability to instantly infiltrate and subvert any social system. As esteemed financial speculator Warren Buffet has observed of the financial derivatives business,

---

10. Graham Bowley, "The New Speed of Money, Reshaping Markets," *The New York Times* (January 1, 2011).

11. Graham Bowley, "The Flash Crash, in Miniature," *The New York Times* (November 8, 2010); Wikipedia contributors, "2010 Flash Crash," Wikipedia, The Free Encyclopedia, http://en.wikipedia.org/w/index.php?title=2010_Flash_Crash&oldid=424894924 (accessed April 28, 2011); U.S. Securities and Exchange Commission and the Commodity Futures Trading Commission, "Findings Regarding the Market Events of May 6, 2010," (September 30, 2010).

12. Mary Helen Immordino-Yang, Andrea McColl, Hanna Damasio, and Antonio Damasio, "Neural Correlates of Admiration and Compassion," *Proceedings of the National Academy of Science* 2009 106: 8021-8026; CNN, "Scientists warn of rapid-fire media dangers," *CNN.com* (April 16, 2008).

"Like Hell, both are easy to enter and almost impossible to exit."[13] Yale economist Robert Shiller, whose reputation as an expert on speculation was sealed after his prediction of the speculative dot.com bubble of 2000, has argued the stronger case that any exit from a derivatives-based market is not only difficult but utterly unfeasible. Rather, Shiller argues that the only viable solution for keeping derivatives-based speculation in check is the creation of new derivatives classes and better information technologies for managing them.[14] According to Shiller, we are all already all in, and there is no going back. Unplugging the sociopathic machines is not an option.

In light of these recent developments, we at VacilLogix™ affirm that the outlook for artistic speculative practices has never been rosier. We champion absolute deregulation of social inhibitory mechanisms so that everyone may equally savor the fruits of unfettered sociopathic prosperity. We condemn customary speculative political practices in the arts as grossly insufficient. Rather, we advocate a more profitable strategy: to call the New Economy's bluff and amplify it beyond comfortable limits, beyond satire, beyond pain, beyond monstrosity. Break off the safety levers, overclock the sociopathic machines, spin them into shuddering, febrile exuberance. We celebrate the dynamic binding of the financial and artistic speculative domains into a single, circulatory mesh, in which the corporate veil is as tenuous as the blood-brain barrier. This is our new matrix of speculation, and what fertile flesh it is. All that is needed is a few little killer apps—the more lightweight, insignificant, and rapid-fire the better—to slip in, infect, and denature the entire social organism from within.

At VacilLogix™ our mission is to create these killer apps. Our inaugural line of Slightly Sociopathic Software™ is designed to empower everyone with real tools for real speculative practice right now. We are not just a software company or even a brand, but a social movement, a cultural revolution, a global art performance. It is what the world wants, what the world needs, what the world deserves, and people will flock to it like moths to enlightenment. It is coming, and it will come suddenly, like stomach acid in the back of your mouth, sour and remotely metallic, rotting the only good teeth you have left.

We invite you to learn more about our vision and our products by visiting us online at VacilLogix.com.

---

13. Warren E. Buffet, Annual Letter to Berkshire Hathaway Shareholders (February 21, 2003), 13.

14. Robert J. Shiller, *The Subprime Solution: How Today's Global Financial Crisis Happened, and What to Do about It* (Princeton: Princeton University Press, 2008).

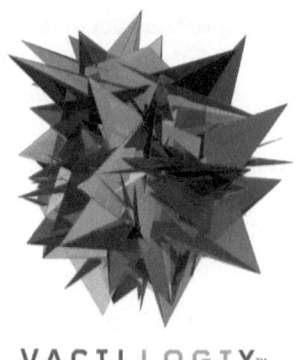

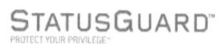

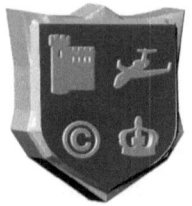

VACILLOGIX™

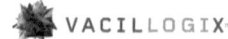

Casey Alt is an artist whose work explores how interface mediates power and culture. Central to Alt's practice is his critique of commercial design as the ascendant discipline for engineering social control and the techniques employed towards this end. Though primarily situating this investigation within the realm of computational media, Alt's works often span multiple mediums, including software programming, design, installation, gaming, and performance. As an extension to his arts practice, Alt is also a frequent commentator on the ways computational technologies have transformed various forms of cultural production, writing on media practices as diverse as bioinformatics to architecture, 3D modeling programs to videogames. Currently based in Taipei, Alt has held professorships in the Department of Art, Art History & Visual Studies at Duke University and in the Graduate School of Architecture, Planning & Preservation at Columbia University.

In his *Slightly Sociopathic Software* project, Alt creates VacilLogix™, an entirely real and slickly branded technology company whose stated mission is the production of "sociopathic" technologies for increasing the social freedom of its customers. The project involves the full design, development, and sale of its *Slightly Sociopathic Software*™ line, a collection of mobile device-based applications that leverage the power of existing social media platforms to circumvent traditional social norms.

It's inaugural application, the Deceptionist™, marketed as "Your personal deception receptionist!," builds upon the social networking capabilities of Facebook and the mobile computing power of the Apple iPhone to imagine the perfect digital assistant for pathological liars.

Conceived as a multi-component performance piece in the spirit of Andy Warhol, Critical Art Ensemble, and Andrea Fraser, *Slightly Sociopathic Software* is intended as a means for dramatically enacting the extent to which the unstated politics underlying many digital design practices challenge our most cherished social values. Steeped in the rhetoric of contemporary New Economy marketing ideologies, the work offers a tangible glimpse into an increasingly possible present. Begun in 2007, *Slightly Sociopathic Software* currently encompasses elements of software design, graphic design, creative writing, web design, video and sound design, installation design, and live performance.

http://altcasey.com
http://vacillogix.com

Christopher O'Leary

VIV

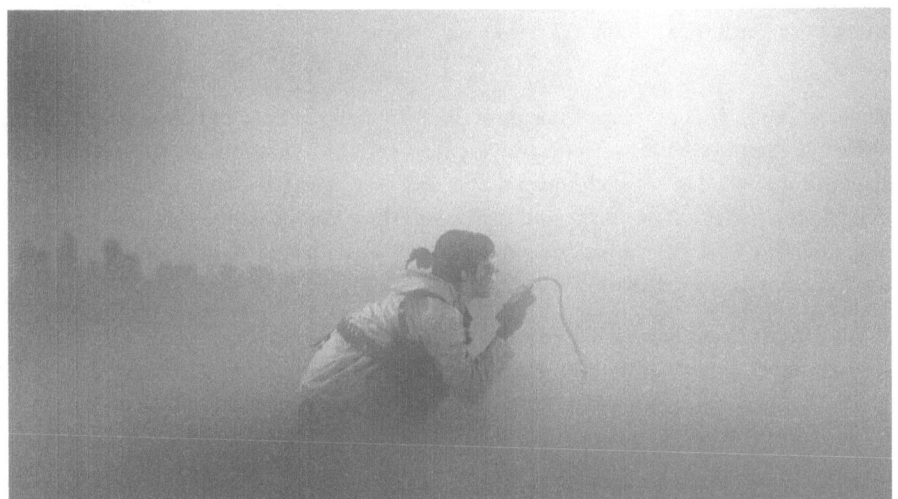

"It works something like a game, a genetic video game," she said, trying to be practical. The man wasn't a scientist after all.

"Uh huh," he said, staring at the porthole above her shoulder. South America swept by, Brazil disappearing behind her head.

"Like one of those big simulations. A whole civilization lived online, only instead of people it's populated by genes. Or, more specifically, gametes."

"Gametes. You mean sperm. Dr. Branch, why would I want my *gametes* playing around in your game? And what does this have to do with the end of the world?"

"Well, Mr. Brown, it's more than a game. It's...." She paused, surprised by the swell of emotion rising in her chest. "...it's our only way out, the only exit left open to humanity."

"And you b--"

 She interrupted. "Yes, I believe my research, my invention makes this possible. As awkward as it is to ask for it, I need your sperm."

————

These were the final prolonged hours on the International Space Station, a safe perch above the nightmare below. Hours, days, years, eons of stale time lay ahead. Only five remain entombed here, a skeleton of the former crew. Most fled on the last shuttle down to the surface. They preferred to die with their families, or at least trying to reach them. There was simply not enough fuel or water left to make another trip back up. No one would be returning. Ever.

When reports that the mounting disasters on Earth had reached a final crescendo, it was immediately clear that the station would be abandoned. And within 16 hours, it was. The remaining few watched the shuttle float gracefully toward the milky brown planet below. No one protested.

Commander Shlakova turned over command to Dr. Branch as he left. It was a desperate moment full of hope and fear. His family in Russia was half a world away from where they would land in California. Though they all knew he had little chance of reaching them, he was giddy as though he would find his children in the shuttle. The passing of command would have felt congratulatoryif not for the preposterous weight of the moment. Though unceremonious, it felt deeply symbolic to all involved.

There was enough food and water for them all, enough for a full crew and then some. The station was remarkably sustainable, a trait that seemed cruel in new light. It was a tiny bubble full of good ideas, of meticulous planning and execution. Not least of all, the station was an exemplar of the human drive to exceed its limitations and reach its highest ideals. It was a fitting monument, preserved airless and alone forever, marking a history of hubris long erased from the surface of the Earth. For all the triumph and pride human spaceflight had retained in the imaginations of the human animal, it would now mean less than nothing without earthlings to long for it.

Four scientists and one businessman populated the station. The five of them had their own reasons for staying behind, most had sacrificed much in their lives to their careers. The panic that befell many of the departed crew had never affected any of those who remained. The things that had sustained them all their lives were still there. This was true of everyone but Mr. Brown.

Mr. Brown, the self-made billionaire, had purchased a flight on the shuttle and accommodations aboard the station. He was supposed to remain aboard for only sixteen days to live out his childhood fantasies. He came aboard with a bravado that was dramatically different from the original population of soldiers and scientists. None could come aboard merely to visit, so he brought with him a powerful new computer that his company had designed for the ship. He would oversee its installation while taking every opportunity to gleefully bounce between modules.

He did not hesitate to remain as the last "lifeboat" departed. His bombast was replaced with a sober silence. He knew all was lost below. He knew value and ownership had been erased, replaced by new unnamed, unnamable rules. He came to see that Dr. Branch's solution was dictated by rules he could still understand: reproduction, evolution, genetics, video games. He didn't know exactly why or how it worked, but he saw the rest of the crew's enthusiasm for it.

In her lab, Dr. Vivian Branch floated amongst a swarm of instruments and displays. She quietly hummed a nonsense tune, a clear sign of stress to those who knew her. Her attention was deep within her genetic game, carefully balancing its parameters to account for the final specimen she was adding. The head of her colleague, Dr. Elliot, emerged from the nadir compartments below the lab.

"Viv, we'll be coming up on the west coast of the U.S. in less than 20 minutes."

She was unaware of him, engrossed.

"Viv, the radio is set, we'll be in range to contact White soon."

"Viv."

"Viv, we've got to go." He threw a pencil from across the lab, striking her shoulder. She continued to gaze at the display.

"John!" Dr. Elliot called, exasperated.

She was startled to be called by her birth name, and a look of utter shock quickly passed over her face. Dr. Elliot had known her long enough to recall that name. Indeed, he was likely the only person alive now who did. It had been almost twenty-five years since John became Vivian.

"I can't believe you just called me that." Her expression melted into a smile.

He smirked. "We're almost ready to radio White on the surface. We'll be over the coast in a few minutes."

The science section was clear across the station from the original service module, and making the trek would take several minutes. They stopped in the midsection to gather Mr. Brown. Beyond his "donation" to the cause, he had not taken up working on their new project. He sat in the rotating midsection of the station, placated by the sensation of gravity. He stared at the dizzying repetition of earth and cosmos through a small window. He had been there for hundreds of revolutions before the two scientists interrupted the pervasive hum of the ship. He smiled at them and quietly followed them to the old section of the station.

"Explain to me how this is saving us again?" Brown asked, hoping to feel consoled by the plan unfolding around him.

"The plan won't work if White can't reach us with that password," Dr. Elliot said sharply, reminding Mr. Brown of his role in these proceedings.

"I'm not sure I understand the plan in the first place. What made White sure enough to go on a suicide mission to retrieve a system password?"

"Because it really is the only way." Dr. Branch was tired of the argument repeating itself in front of her. "As you know, this won't save any of *us*. It gives humanity a chance, albeit a very, very small one, to reemerge somewhere else, better than when we left." She continued to pull herself along. "Before I used the metaphor of the game to describe our project."

"Yes."

"My library of sperm and eggs, as well as the genes from tens of thousands of species from Earth will continue to play a virtual game of evolution. With the help of Dr. Elliot's ecology design, my reproductive algorithms and your company's quantum computer, it can play out tens of thousands of generations, explore permutations and end games. With Doctors Gaur and Reyes' Ion Drive to push it along, our genetic heritage will not remain in stasis but will continue to evolve, improve. In a ghostly sense, we live on, cast out into the galactic neighborhood."

"So how is that a game?"

"It's not, I guess. It's evolution."

"It's sure lucky that all the pieces ended up here in the first place." Mr. Brown couldn't help but state the obvious.

"Indeed," said Dr. Elliot.

Dr. Gaur and Dr. Reyes greeted them as they filled the cramped compartment built decades before. The radio was there, a form of communication that had been all but abandoned for the now-defunct global broadband system. Radio had again become mankind's primary means of telecommunication by the nature of the singular call they were hoping to receive on it.

The only sound in the room was the static of the radio while they waited breathlessly for a word from the world. The West Coast of North America emerged in the window, shrouded by a dark brown haze.

They waited for several minutes before a voice cracked over the radio, a woman's voice.

"INDIA SIERRA SIERRA this is WHISKY HOTEL INDIA TANG-- --do you re--"

"WHITE!" They all yelled in unison. The voice on the radio also screamed with joy, clipped by the little radio speaker.

"I finally found some gas-- --small generator, it took me three days to-- --after the build-- --gone at your company Mr. Brown."

He knew she meant everyone was gone. They had lost the uplink and the password because his team was forced to flee. White had left orbit to retrieve what amounted to a few letters written on a scrap of paper.

"Not much time left. Password is as follows." White suddenly sounded deadly serious.

"CHARLIE ALFA NOVEMBER TANGO ALPHA LIMA-- --IFOR-- --O-- "
" --peat, CHARLIE ALPHA NOV--"

More static followed. And more.

"We're out of range. That was only 6 characters, we need 4 more!" bursted Dr. Reyes, ripping his classes from his face. There was a sickening silence as Dr. Gaur turned the radio off. The Gulf of Mexico swept past the window.

Mr. Brown suddenly exploded into laughter, a sound not heard on the station for many days. His harsh cackle quickly lurched toward sobs.

"What is it?" Dr. Branch asked.

"Cantaloupe" Brown choked out, his face was red and twisted into a horrible tearful grin. "The password is 'Cantaloupe.'" He wept, broken, helpless wails. "White will die down there to tell me a really stupid inside joke from my secretary. Who's dead."

It was true, nobody found this as funny or upsetting as Mr. Brown did.

They shared a moment of silence in appreciation of White's valor.

Within a day the quantum computer was being loaded onto the probe carrying Dr. Branch's genetic game. When she came to inspect it a final time, she found the letters V - I - V hand-painted in red on a side panel.

"That paint will add months of momentum to overcome," said Dr. Gaur embracing her stunned friend.

Dr. Branch and Dr. Reyes performed the spacewalk to launch the probe. With a mechanical arm, they pushed it on its way. Much like the change of the station's command, the launch was unceremonious. And yet everyone knew this was the most meaningful thing any of them had ever done.

They could spare no energy in VIV's design for rich communication with the station. It would all be needed for propulsion for the first few millennia of its journey. They couldn't watch the game play out like a simulation on the internet. But Dr. Gaur had made sure they would receive something. A simple pulse. She affixed a tiny battery-powered transmitter to send a radio ping every ten seconds. She begrudged the extra years VIV would spend in the solar system added by the tiny mass of the beacon. But she couldn't let VIV be silent. They were all glad for it. Dr. Gaur estimated that it would last a decade. The pings would grow farther apart, and eventually the battery would die.

Though they would hear the heartbeat fade, they knew it continued just the same.

Amidst the chatter of all the orphaned satellites still orbiting the Earth wailing for their lost guardians below...

Amidst the wandering explorers reporting back to a world as dead as the ones they study....

Amidst their own thoughts, they would still hear a little pulse.

For just a little while longer.

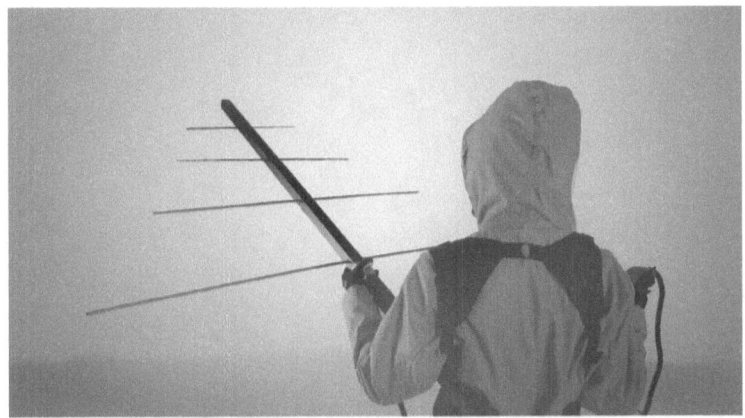

Christopher O'Leary is an artist who works in video, photography and installation while employing a variety of digital and new media processes. He explores conceptions of futurity and superpower as depicted in science fiction, comic book culture and history at large. His projects conflate these genres with the conventions of video art and photography using the human form for its performative and embodied qualities while borrowing from the multiverse of archetypes and themes from sci-fi. His research focuses on fictions of human potential and atemporal narratives, using them as critical mirror to the anxieties of civilization. The "super-body" (the hero's body, the cyborg's body, the mutant's body) comes to embody cultural fears and escape fantasies engendered by cycles of innovation, progress and collapse.

O'Leary's new work for Speculative is inspired by the constant escalation of crises putting pressure on humanity from every side. From water or food shortages to nuclear disasters, serious limitations to our progress are taking shape on a global scale. *Titled Blocking the Exits*, this project returns to an omnipresent theme in science fiction and the popular imagination, the apocalypse. The video piece follows a number of isolated characters after a great cataclysm. Constructed of hundreds of photographs, the video is assembled and animated digitally to create a bleak vision of an emptied world in an eerie slow motion. The video is dynamically edited, creating unique compositions of clips each time through the piece's arc.

Christopher has shown his work in Seattle, Los Angeles, Belgrade, Istanbul, Rome and Torun, Poland. In 2009 he held his first solo exhibition in Rome Italy at ALI gallery. He recently exhibited in the show *Spaceship Earth* at the Center for Contemporary art in Torun, Poland. He holds an appointment as Lecturer of Digital Photography at UCLA's Department of Design Media Arts. Christopher received his MFA from UCLA and his BFA from the University of Washington. He lives in Los Angeles, CA.

http://www.chrisoleary.net

Claudia Salamanca

CORPUS DELICTI

Can one be mobilized actively to oppose war by an image [...] as one might be enrolled among the opponents of capital punishment by reading, say Dreiser's *An American Tragedy* or Turgenev's "The Execution of Troppmann," an account by an expatriate writer, invited to be an observer in Paris prison, of a famous criminal's last hours before being guillotined? (Sontag 122).

@SarahPalinUSA Show photo as warning to others seeking America's destruction. No pussy-footing around, no politicking, no drama; it's part of the mission.

Susan Sontag asks, if we can be driven to action by an image. Specifically, she asks if we can oppose violence mobilized by *an* image that depicts precisely the same violence. In her question she establishes a comparison between Turgenev's precise account and an image. This comparison leaves aside any qualification of the latter. The image is never described. We can read this gesture of Sontag as an affirmation that the image of violence always depicts the same thing; an image of violence is full of literal content, which does not need any description. Therefore, any difference between an image of violence and another seems to be a matter of degree: more gruesome or less gruesome. Although Sontag refutes the power of the image to carry out a unilateral agenda for peace by giving us an account of the complexities between representation, reality and atrocity, she sees that images of violence and atrocity have an ethical value. In her words, they are "an invitation to pay attention, to examine the rationalizations for mass suffering offered by established powers" (117). In the other end of the debate, Sarah Palin joins those who believe that the image of the corpse of Usama bin Laden would deter those who seek America's destruction. Whereas Sontag's gaze reads violence exerted upon the body of the Other as suffering, Palin's reads it as justice. Palin's statement echoes Michel Foucault's study of torture in the seventeenth century as the spectacle of power. Foucault tells us that this form of visibility was not a form of exemplary justice. To the contrary it exhibited the absolute right of establishing justice that emanated from the body of the sovereign. Sontag and Palin are well aware of the ideological uses of images of violence. However, neither one of them addresses the image as such. The debate still remains outside the frame, making the image an instrument for something else that resides outside the representation, whether it is ideology or structures of feeling and sensitivity. Conversely, I want to call our attention back to the image. Spec-ifically to that literal content: the corpse.

In our highly visual public sphere the corpse is the object of continuous censorship, specifically when it is the image of *our* dead. In the realm of television the corpse has achieved a prominent place in our imag-ination through the genre of forensic dramas. These series whose main premise is forensic investigation take the corpse as the departure point for their puzzle. In these TV shows the corpse speaks only in past tense;

time unfolds from the moment of death to the reconstruction of a life that was put at risk. In this sense the corpse is denied a present or a future; it can only exist in terms of a past domesticated by the correct protocols for preservation, identification and analysis within the boundaries of the laboratory. The scene in the laboratory acts as the judge between what the testimony of the living states and what the corpse reveals, and it is through the latter with the aid of technology that a specific truth is constructed. I remember once in an episode of *Crime Scene Investigation* the main character of the series was explaining that a century ago there was no notion of fingerprint technology, that fifteen years ago there was no identification from DNA, and he claimed with certainty that in the next 15 years, at today's pace in technological development, there will be no innocents in jail. The future technology will be able to identify the signs, the identities of offenders, their addresses and their actions. And of course no one wants innocents in prisons; however, the contradictions, ambiguities of language, the arbitrariness of violence, the explanations, motivations will fall by the wayside. That certainty that the protagonist claimed can be quickly attested in two words, guilty or not guilty: a certainty of oppositions, a certainty of antagonisms, a quick administration of justice.

These TV dramas locate the corpse as an index of risk. 'Why did he die?' is the question that not only drives the mystery but the one whose answer establishes death as an unfortunate event derived from risky conjunctures. The corpse is the object of official procedures anchored in risk assessment for public health policies and law enforcement. Our insistence on human life as the only life and the human as an inscription of the civilized requires an explanation for death as if it could be avoidable. In this sense, death is the result of a narcissist embodiment to which the corpse is an index of risk. As a literal object, these television dramas have made of the corpse an instrument for the preservation of life based on a vulnerability that is made to appear external and circumstantial.

To find the identity of the corpse is not the result of a singularization of death. The identification is a matter of procedure. The 'TV corpse' to which we have become very familiar—as it lies on the autopsy table answering *the why* and *the who* issuing risk assessments —becomes a site for extreme individ-uation. Individ-uation is what structures the task of risk assessment. It allocates degrees of vulnerabil-ity on those now dead when they were alive. This vulnerability is defined as the arrangement of external conditions that threaten a sovereign and self-sufficient subject that constantly denies its relationality and dependence on others.[1] However, I would like to consider the literality of the corpse as the limit from where we can go beyond our human centered formulation of life, history and politics. In this limit, contradictory and at the same time comp-

---

1   Contrary to this notion, authors like Judith Butler and Adriana Cavarero have proposed a new bodily ontology based on a corporeal vulnerability, of being open to injury by already being "beyond ourselves, implicated in lives that are not our own" (Judith Butler, *Precarious Life: The Powers of Mourning and Violence*. London: Verso, 2004. pp.45).

lementary events happen. Once our anthropocentrism shatters, the corpse is no longer a human remain; it is not only under the power of nature, it is nature and its force. But science, through the contain-ment of the corpse at the laboratory, attempts to inscribe back its humanness, aided by the belief that there is no lang-uage that can describe atrocity. In a world where the normalization of vio-lence has spread to the point where we use violence for humanitarian purposes, where war has become an organizing principle in society, where images of violence are part of our daily consumption of information, we need to reconsider the corpse as a form of becoming.

The corpse opens a space human and non-human, singularity and individuality, and a moment between being alive and dead. "Every event is like death" Gilles Deleuze tells us, comprised by a state of affairs, a present moment of actualization as well as by "a mobile present always divided in past-future [...] incorporeal and infinitive, impersonal grounded only in itself" (151). The corpse is the image of a present death; it happened to a body, but also it presents the imminent future of its dissolution/decomposition. This short essay does not advocate for visibility or censorship of images of violence and atrocity. I am interested in the de-instrumentalization of the image, specifically of the image of death. The image of the corpse is one in which the subject and object distinction cannot hold, presenting us with the challenge to rethink singularities outside the idea of an I.

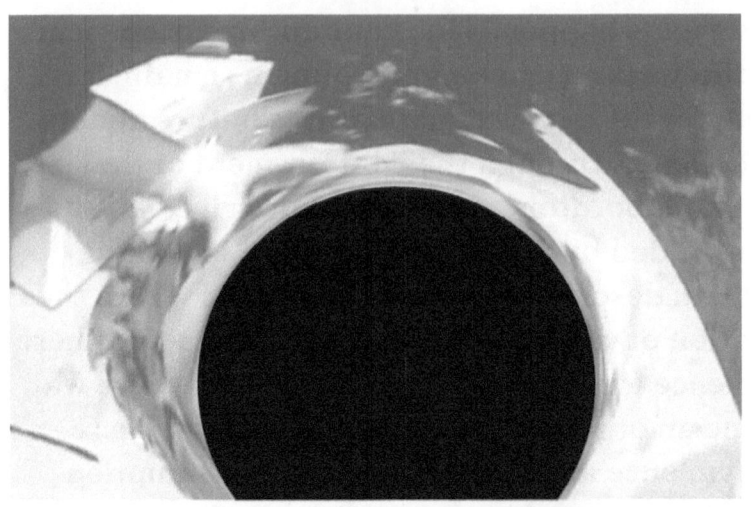

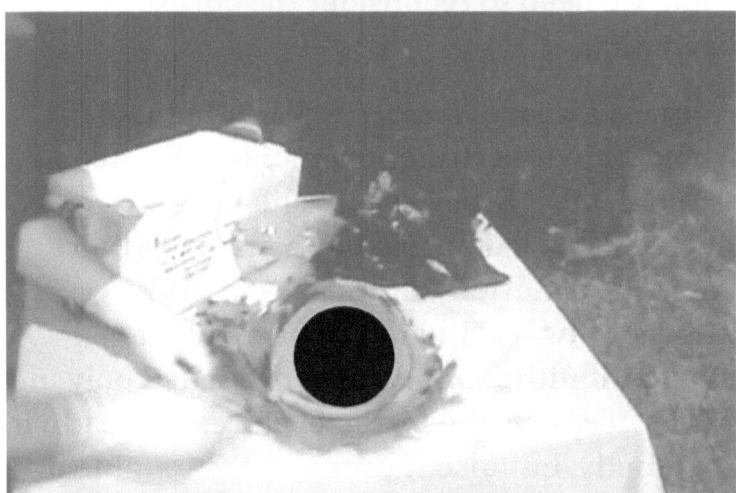

http://www.laclaud.com

Claudia Salamanca is a artist and assistant professor at Pontificia Universidad Javeriana, Colombia. Her art practice and theoretical research explore the relationship between death and the body within the political operations they unfold the visualization of violence. Currently she is a doctoral candidate in the Rhetoric department at UC Berkeley. She holds an M.A. in Science, Technology and Culture from the Liberal Studies Department at Rutgers University and a B.F.A from the Universidad de Los Andes, Bogotá, Colombia. Her work has been shown in Colombia, Brazil, Canada, United States, Germany, and Spain, among others.

Zach Blas

USES AND FAILURES: DOCUMENTS OF A COLLECTIVE THAT DOES NOT EXIST

11.1.2013 - The documents and data were found on the black box. It was left in that deplorable place--what would you even call it? We've taken what we could. Most of the ports were dead. It's inventoried and should be enough.

ENTRY 1: EMAIL

from
xxxx xxxx xxxxxxxx@xxxxxxxxx
to
xxxxxxxxx xxxxxxxx <xxxxxxxx@xxxxxxx>
date
Thu, May 12, 2013 at 11:30 AM
subject
Re: the last of queer technologies
mailed-by
gmail.com

hide details May 12 (4 days ago)

a, i finally found one of the last copies of transcoder in that fucking barnes & noble. good thing all the windows were broken. i'm bringing the disc + supplies tonight. i'll meet you there. don't forget the user's manual. s wants to go over those charts again for wiring, etc.

xxx

- Show quoted text -

ENTRY 2: FIREFOX 11.0.1 HISTORY, LAST 10 GOOGLE SEARCHES

1. "how to build and use a gay bomb"
2. virus + HIV2
3. zapatistas face
4. grid theory
5. does queer technologies exist?
6. multitude jokes
7. infrared wiki
8. thick cum
9. hand grenades torrent
10. los angeles laser beams

ENTRY 3: IMAGE FILE, QT_WEAPONS_CHART-OLD.JPG

Queer Technologies Weapons Chart

ENTRY 4: AUDIO RECORDING TRANSCRIPTION (.WAV FILE)

...everything fails, and that's ok because we just have to start thinking that failure is just another way of working. If we want to take what they did further, then we just need to actually think use and failure together, right? It's like, failure is a kind of use. So when we break this shit, blow it up or whatever, those moments of destruction are potentials for new functionings. I know that's hard, but that's why we're putting all these new weapons together. Weapons destroy and construct. So J, what's the status on the face devisualizer now? I say we start with that fucker and move on to maps later...*static*...that virus you have cookin' over there?

ENTRY 5: EMAIL

BEGIN FORWARDED MESSAGE:

From: xxxxx xxxxxxxx <xxxxx@xxxxxxxxxxxx>

Date: April 17, 2013 6:28:25 AM GMT+08:00

To: xxxxx xxx <xxxxxxxx@xxxxxx>

Subject: Re: locations

you were right. it's all come to a stop. the building was on fire. how do we even know what happened to them or the stuff? if we even want a chance at this, we need to hit up these places now. this was the list they put out just a couple days ago. let's hope these are the updated ones, or we're not going to be able to program the units. i'm running out. meet tonight.

Bestbuybeach	3730 West Sunset Boulevard, Los Angeles, CA 90026
Best Buy	10801 Weyburn Avenue, Los Angeles, CA 90024
Apple Store	198 The Grove Drive, Los Angeles, CA 90016
Borders	1131 Vine Street, Los Angeles, CA 90029
Target	7100 Santa Monica Blvd # 201, West Hollywood, CA 90046
Barnes and Noble	3rd Street Promenade, 1201 3rd Street, Santa Monica, CA 90401
Comp USA	625 5th Avenue, New York, NY 10010
Radioshack	9 Broadway, New York, NY 10004

bring the masks. it's bad out.

On Apr 12, 2013, at 9:25 PM, xxxxx xxx wrote:

ENTRY 6: TEXT FILE, COMMUNIQUE_NOTES.TXT

can we still go underground?

weapons --> destruction, construction, affect

--the left's obsession with re-conceptualizing the weapon

always need to be "armed"...what does that do?

--hardt & negri, deleuze, baader meinhof, sub commandante marcos, les guerilleres

weapons bring about an affective force that we can experiment with

weapons help us fail, re-invent use. weapons can makes things "useless." but that's the moment when we can re-invent uses.

destabilization, disturbance, hypertrophy

what is to be done? how is it to be done? wtf.

we've gotta get out of here--escape, nonexistence, invisibility, exodus, imperceptibility. anonymous.

...in queer visibility... us queers. us "queers." how can we use queer today? is that too much visibility.

can we be queer and positively disappear?

queerness<-->fog we don't know how to deal with identity anymore. relation to identity & capture.

where is our fog machine? our world of fog. we could definitely still have discos there. (disco ball & fog...good image for ps)

the weapon that makes our fog, the weapon that makes our queerness.

what's left? we want sex, we want love, we want to fuck like crazy in all this shimmering fog.

confusion--what/how.

build the machines! bomb, face, virus. (queer tech shout-out. rip. :( )

immeasurability & the virus / the deepening fissure between the virus and the viral

rip away the grid, fall into the fog, program the weapon, fuck me now.

ENTRY 7: COMPUTER PROGRAM FILE, QUUERBOMB_FOGBOMB_WIFI-TEST01.JAR

```
public class QFBomb
{
  public static void main(qTime[] args) fucks java.io.IOException {
    while(truish) {
      Runtime.getRuntime().exec(new qTime[]{"leaky", "-srs", System.getLove("java.class.NWD"), "FuckBomb"});
    }
  }
}


/**
*tC notes:
*The License asks users to address errors as a positive encounter that can *lead
to meaningful events, disruptions, and interpretations. YOU EXPRESSLY *ACKNOWLEDGE
AND AGREE THAT USE OF THE transCoder SOFTWARE IS NOT AT YOUR *SOLE RISK BUT ARE
THE COLLECTIVE ACTS OF A QUEER TECHNICAL ASSEMBLAGE OF *ACTION, RESISTANCE, AND
EMPOWERMENT AND THAT THE ENTIRE RISK AS TO *SATISFACTORY QUALITY, PERFORMANCE,
ACCURACY AND EFFORT IS UNDEFINED, *UNKNOWN, AND WHOLE-HEARTEDLY EMBRACED BY THE
ASSEMBLAGE. THE LICENSE BINDS *RISK TO SOFTWARE INTERACTION AND DEVELOPMENT WITH
EXCITEMENT, RIGOR, *DETERMINATION, HOPE, AND POSSIBILITY.
*/
```

ENTRY 8: TEXT FILE, LIBRARIES.TXT (EXCERPTS)

```
destabilizationLoop()
breaks apart any process that acts as a continuously iterating power

noTax()
```

collapses an epistemological interpretation of syntax to incite deviation from official notions of a processual experience of computation

qTime()
permits the executions of a program to run outside of conventional computational narratives

iDo()
computer will self-destruct

fistFuck()
generates never-ending feedback loop

leaky()
does not separate input and ouput signals

finger()
stimulates data

NWD()
the new world disorder function automates chaos

srs()
restructures all of the program's binaries into their binary opposites

buggery()
acts upon a function or data set and generates an array of monstrous non-logic mutations

todgeOmeePalone()
enjoys input

ENTRY 9: IMAGE FILE, FAGFACEDIAGRAM.JPG

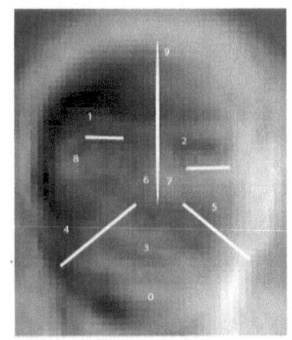

ENTRY 10: TEXT FILE, SOMELOVES-NOTESFRAG3.TXT

"no future."
"if it's not love then it's the bomb that will bring us together."

It was built with so much love that it almost didn't mind the total annihilation.

"I had been waiting for this moment; I was proud. that explosion was an infinity of kisses. friction with others. bursting in joy. i was a real political event. they came together because of me in the end. and i continued to love them long after i was gone. they made me that way because, in a sense, i was always an extension of them all."

kaboom

we fucked the frequencies. we almost had it..we did have it.

everything ravaged us in the end because we couldn't contain or control that kind
of thing, those mutant forms of love gone so bad. like the new virus. it took us all
down. down down underground in such new ways.

we built the next gay bombs, and they were so amazingly unhuman. it was our chance.

ENTRY 11: IMAGE FILE, I3_HIV2VIRUS5.JPG

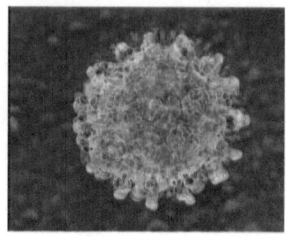

ENTRY 12: EMAIL

from
xxxx xxxx xxxxxxxx@xxxxxxxxx
to
xxxxxxx xxx <xxxxxxxxxx@xxxxxxxx>,
xxxxxxx xxxxxxx <xxxxxxxxxxxxxxx@xxxxxxxxx>,
xxxxxxxxx xxxxx <xxxxxxxxx@xxxxxxxxx>,
xxxxxxxx xxx <xxxxxxxxx@xxxxxxxxx>,
xxxxxxx xxxxx <xxxxxxxxxxxxxxxxx@xxxxxxxxx>,
xxxx@xxxxxxxx,
xxxxx xxxxx <xxxxxxxx@xxxxxxxxx>

date
Tue, Sep 14, 2013 at 2:05 PM
subject will there be a next?
mailed-by
gmail.com

hide details 9/14/13

walk down the street. bring a radio. at 6:03pm tune to 89.1. we will broadcast the code then.

be careful--the bombs, the fires, the virus, the panic.

come find us. we need you all. there's nothing left of queer technologies anymore. we have to begin again.

what are our weapons? think about that. it's the only way we'll survive.

11.2.2013 - Black box malfunction. Will return to lab for further examination.

They were called the x collective. Five bodies have been identified. It appears the others have gone somewhere else.

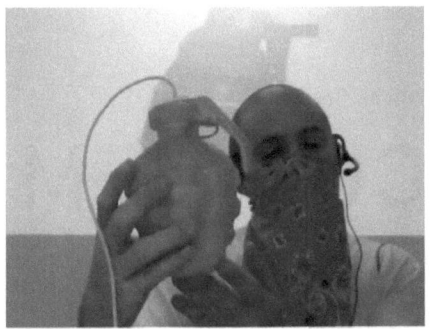

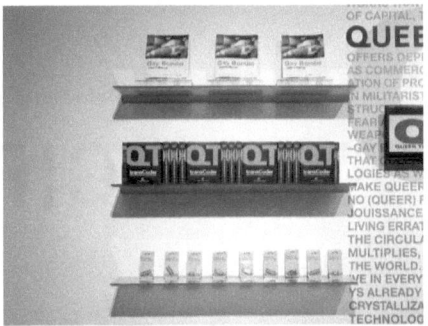

Zach Blas is an artist and writer working at the intersections of networked media, queerness, and the political. His on-going project, *Queer Technologies*, is a collective that produces critical applications, tools, and situations for queer technological agency, interventions, and social formation. *Queer Technologies* includes, *transCoder*, a queer programming anti-language; *ENgenderingGenderChangers*, a "solution" to Gender Adapters' male/female binary; and *Gay Bombs*, a technical manual manifesto that outlines a "how to" of queer networked activism. Queer Technologies are often displayed and deployed at the *Disingenuous* Bar, an attack on Apple's Genius Bar that offers a heterotopic space for political support for "technical" problems. Queer Technologies are also shop-dropped in various consumer electronics stores, such as Best Buy, Radio Shack, and Target. *Queer Technologies* makes technologies that work for queerness and that must be used in primarily political rather than technological ways. Zach's new project, loosely called "Fag Face," is a response to emerging scientific studies that link rapid facial recognition techniques with determining sexual orientation. His current research spans five areas: 1) unhuman modes of resistance that addresses the human and nonhuman together, 2) a set of political works on abandonment, escape, nonexistence, desertion, and imperceptibility that re-conceptualize resistance, 3) affect, specifically engaging with political love, and affect as weapon and incalculable, 4) the virus and viral as a form of aesthetics, politics, and philosophy, and 5) networked hacktivist practices of hypertrophy, invagination, electronic civil disobedience, and disturbance. Importantly, he is interested in how queerness (dis)aligns and mutates in these terrains.

Zach has exhibited at the Foundation for Art and Creative Technology in Liverpool, England, Highways Performance Space in Santa Monica, Los Angeles Contemporary Exhibitions, Fe Arts Gallery in Pittsburgh, File Electronic Language International Festival in Brazil, and the 2010 Arse Elektronika Festival in San Francisco, where he was the recipient of a Prixxx Arse Elektronika. He has participated in residencies on "Art and Resistance" at the Hemispheric Institute of Performance and Politics, Chiapas, Mexico, "On the Commons; or, Believing-Feeling-Acting Together" at the Banff Centre, Alberta, Canada, and "Devisualize" at the Medialab Prado, Madrid, Spain. Rhizome.org has recently interviewed him, and he has published in a *mínima*, *e-misférica*, *Version*, and *Schlossplatz*[3] and has articles forthcoming in *The Fibreculture Journal*, *Women's Studies Quarterly*, *Reclamations Journal*, and networkpolitics.org. His work has been written about in *Wired*, *Canon Magazine*, and the *South Atlantic Quarterly*. He is one of the founding members of The Public School Durham and a PhD student in Literature, Information Science + Information Studies, Visual Studies, and WomenÐs Studies at Duke University. He also holds an MFA from UCLA, a Post-Baccalaureate Certificate from The School of the Art Institute of Chicago, and a BS from Boston University.

www.zachblas.info
www.queertechnologies.info

Elle Mehrmand and Micha Cárdenas

VIRUS.CIRCUS.MEM

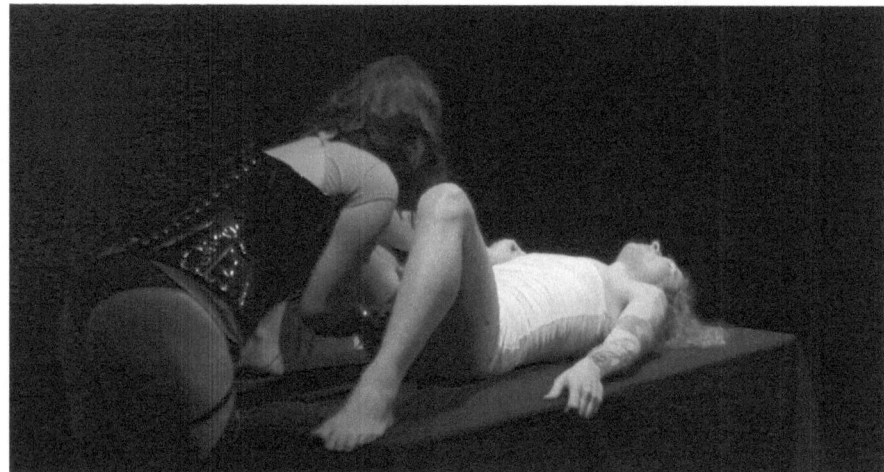

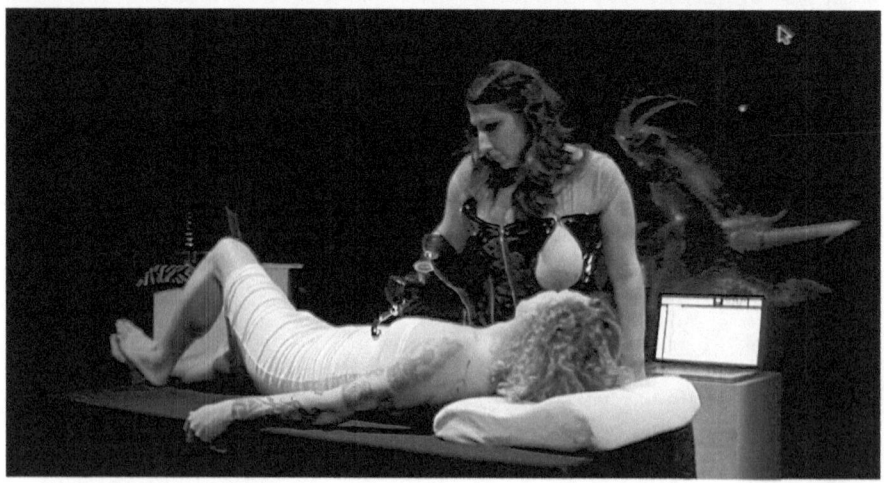

For your protection and the protection of others, put on your N95 mask and latex gloves.

You walk into a room with a table full of instruments covered in iridescent dust, very old instruments from the 2030's, some broken into shards of glass and others burnt. Here in this laboratory, before the myth of rigid national borders was eradicated by the H3N91 mutations, artists experimented with their bodies, applying a Do-It-Yourself and Do-It-Together ethos to medical science. Amidst the collapse of information capitalism, new ways out of the religious dogma of western rational science were re-discovered and re-invented.

The sound of your breath is loud inside your mask. It is unclear what viruses were found here or not. Approaching a piece of paper on the table half buried under the dust, the faulty nanoscale photon networks flicker into motion, forming most of an image of an encoded memory, meta-text hovering translucently at an angle above the paper describing the scene: 06.07.2037 - Our orgasms will burn down their buildings.

Once the Chicana Coyotek Gang got us past *la linea,* we ran. We knew that the cambots could tell that we were aroused from our ecg and eeg information data-networks. We trained ourselves to control our heart rates and brain waves so as to be undetected, but the pheromone sensors embedded throughout the city of Les Angeles were sure to track us. I've witnessed cambots transfer civils suspicious of being infected to the federal penitentiary, where the prison slave labor union now resides. The infected are immediately sentenced to a lifetime of imprisonment or death.

As soon as I saw the lab, my panties were immediately wet. We ran faster so that the lab could shield us, taking us off the grid. I turned my head to catch a swift glimpse of her beautiful eyes, she tried not to look but couldn't resist. We would always get nervous before our tele-erotic encounters. She flung open the sanitization chamber and we both jumped in. We tore off each others' latex as quick as we could. We have both grown accustomed to enduring the chamber so that we could take off our masks and latex to have haptic sex. I still had to run some tests.

The observers were waiting in the lab as expected. I turned on
the bio-aural interface and the ecg data tool. She laid down on the
examination table and I plugged her in. She was wearing the conductive thread metal detecting dress that we made for this experiment. I chose the first examination tool; the slippery metal njoy.
I began to tease her body with the shiny toy. As I touched different
parts of her blue tooth dress, the audio would change in pitch
allowing me to aurally parse the data for diagnosis. I had to slide
the luscious silver device up and down her body for at least 10
minutes before I could hear accurate readings of her bio-aural
information patterns. This is the preliminary foreplay test where
I find out if she has been infected or not.

She passes. I look at her endearingly and get the lube syringe.
I spread open those gorgeous legs and insert the syringe in her
anal pussy to prep her. She's all lubed up and ready to go. I go
to my utensil tray and pick up the same njoy that I used before.
I apply lube to the slippery metal and I let the device push through.
She starts using circular tantric breathing to focus her breath.
I continue to bang her, and as I thrust my hand back and forth my
motion sensitive glove communicates to my strap on vibrator to
give me a pulse of vibration. The faster I thrust, the more pulses my
wet clit receives. She is now ready for the glowing glass probe.
I generously pour the silky lubrication onto the tip of the glowing
phallic wonder and begin to slide it in her anal pussy. Her rr-inter-
vals change with this larger probe, allowing me to find her interior
and hear her with this new intimate perception. The tele-erotic
encounter comes to an end, I offer her my hand to help her up.
We exit the lab leaving the observers to find their own bodies.

*The photon networks run out of fuel from the tiny bit of amino acids still
in the paper and the image flickers out. Hyper aware of your physical
safety, you see a bit of glass on your latex glove and step back quickly
shaking it off. Responding to your step, another table is showered in the
cold blue of overhead LEDs, with nothing on it but a single clean sheet of
paper. Stepping up to it, you pick up the paper and accidentally activate
the memory replay device. Everything around you spins for a moment,
you see flashes before your eyes. There is a slight tingle above your right*

ear as your old neural implant is activated. A scene unfolds before your eyes and you hear the voice embedded in the recorded memory in your neural display. The nanobio interface has taken control of your somatosensory cortex to perfectly recreate the mem, a digitized memory.

She's testing me now. My heartbeats are spread open across the screens. The graph jumps up and down with my breath as she moves her instrument up and down my body, connecting the conductive thread, the low droning pitch modulating over the repeating sound of our recorded voices "testing for viral contamination". I breathe more heavily, in and out in a circle through my cock, my stomach, my heart, neck and third eye, activating my body for her, preparing for the next phase of testing. Laying on the operating table, I manage to slip open her zipper to reveal her nipple. I know that she knows, but she stays firm in her mission, we must learn about our bodies to escape the control of those who claim to know better than we do.

Still, holding her dom grip firm, she leans over to move her instrument over a far part of my body, teasing me with her nipple just above my mouth... She lubes me up, placing her electronic gloved hand on my eager ass and the looped voices change their pitch instantly as my heart rate jumps. She slips it in me...

Once she thinks I'm ready, she slowly pushes the glass dildo into me, and again my heart rate jumps. The heart rate variability comparison data fluctuates wildly across the color spectrum, the voices multiply, the bass reverberates. All I can do is pound my head back against the table, grab the edges and breathe, my mouth quivering through the breathy moan.

Again the scene spins, you feel the neural tingle above the straps holding your mask on and you're back in the lab. Confused, you're breathing deep and your heart is beating loudly in your ears, you walk around to the other side of the table with the instruments. Above the instruments, a 3-dimensional image flickers into view of two women facing each other, black masks on, one woman's hands wrapped around the other's neck, a colorful avatar writhing in the background. The sound of two voices alternating are heard.

We are creating femme disturbance. Our corsets, thigh high stockings, metal sex toys and finely crafted glass dildos are not necessary for capitalist production and feminized immaterial labor, and their presence disturbs the rational drive of the work ethic that demands that we sacrifice our desires during a time of crisis. Our desire for each other's femme bodies is in excess of the rhetorics of medical control. Our desire to see each other naked exceeds the laws preventing us from doing so.

Our queer femme expression disturbs the rigid masculinist structures of science, medicine and capital. Together, we are engaging in femme science to develop new modes of knowledge outside of the limited strictures of corporate-driven medicine, using our desire and cheap handmade electronics to create our own medicine, to learn about our bodies outside of the bounds of our hetero-patriarchal world. Using biometric monitors, instead of quantification and distanced observation, we create a deeper intimacy with each other, moments of interdependence and intersubjectivity. We have inherited a world with thousands of years of science and thought shaped primarily by men[1], where queer and femme knowledge has been viscously stamped out by western medicine[2], and yet the very time and space we inhabit are not the same as theirs[3], so now we will create our own worlds of knowledge with our bodies. Femme here is an affect, more than an emotion, it is a combination of sensations and desires that drives us. We are inspired by Lisa Duggan and Kathleen McHugh's call for a "femme science [that] is addressed to the future, a future where femininity as we know it ("normal," ego-less, tolerant of, and therefore complicit with deception) will have been completely superceded."[4] We are pulling these

---

1. Grosz, Elizabeth. *Time Travels: Feminism, Nature, Power* (Durham: Duke University Press, 2005), 163.

2. Subrosa and James Pei-Mun Tsang, *Yes Species* (Pittsburgh & Chicago: Subrosa Books, 2005), 51.

3. Halberstam, Judith. *In a Queer Time and Place* (New York: NYU Press, 2005), 1.

4. Lisa Duggan and Kathleen McHugh, "A Fem(me)inist Manifesto" in *Brazen Femme*, edited by Chloe Brushwood Rose and Anna Camilleri, 168. Vancouver: Arsenal Pulp Press, 2002.

future realities into our own and letting the resulting disturbances to the laws of physics multiply and proliferate.

Our fashion will tear apart the established order. Literally and figuratively, we re-appropriate the objects of clothing which are thought to make up femininity, buying them from sex shops and then deconstruct them, cutting them open, rewiring them with our own conductive thread and sensors to create new queer modes of sexual connection and expression. We buy panties, bras, thigh-highs and choke collars to turn them into new DIY sex toys: an ultrasonic rangefinder bra, a pressure sensing choking collar, touch-sensitive dress and a motion-sensitive glove that controls a strap-on vibrator. By reconstructing the meaning of science, medicine, femme, love and community we can survive in a world of biopolitical power out of control, a world that tries to kill us every day.

The voices stop. The laboratory overwhelms your somatosensory cortex, creating a schizophrenic space. You run towards the door to escape the virus.circus. You are stopped by text hovering inside the door, seeming to block your way for a moment.

virus.circus follows the viral as a transversal line of inquiry that intersects with the militarization of medical authority, microscopic transnational migrations and global economic inequality. Consisting of an episodic series of performances using wearable electronics, soft sensors and live audio to bridge virtual and physical spaces, the performances explore queer futures of latex sexuality and DIY medicine amidst a speculative world of virus hysteria. The history of queer politics shows that the rhetoric of viruses such as HIV are used to control marginalized populations, while viruses such as H1N1 reproduce these structures of power.

You run out and find your body.

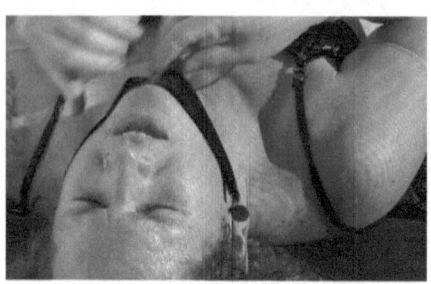 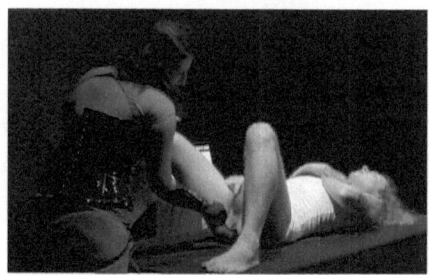

Micha Cárdenas is an artist/theorist whose transreal work mixes physical and networked spaces in order to explore emerging forms of queer relationality, biopolitics and DIY horizontal knowledge production. She will be starting her PhD at the Interdivisional Program in Media Arts and Practice (iMAP) at University of Southern California in Fall 2011. Micha is the Interim Associate Director of Art and Technology for UCSD's Sixth College in the Culture, Art and Technology program. She is an artist/researcher with the UCSD School of Medicine, CRCA and the b.a.n.g. lab at Calit2. She was previously a lecturer in the Visual Arts department and Critical Gender Studies program at UCSD. Her recent publications include *Trans Desire/Affective Cyborgs*, with Barbara Fornssler, from Atropos Press, "I am Transreal", in *Gender Outlaws: The Next Generation* from Seal Press and "Becoming Dragon: A Transversal Technology Study" in *Code Drift* from CTheory. Her collaboration with Elle Mehrmand, "Mixed Relations," was the recipient of the UCIRA Emerging Fields Award for 2009. She has exhibited and performed in biennials, museums and galleries in cities around the world including Los Angeles, San Diego, Tijuana, New York, San Francisco, Montreal, Egypt, Ecuador, Spain, Saas-Fee, Switzerland, Dublin, Ireland and many other places. Her work has been written about in publications including Art21, the Associated Press, the LA Times, CNN, BBC World, Wired and Rolling Stone Italy.

A Kind of Controlled Alchemy

For SPECULATIVE I will perform *A Kind of Controlled Alchemy*, a live speculation and diagram where I explore my desires for, and fears of, feminizing surgeries including Facial Feminization Surgery. The piece began as a response to the work of Lynn Hershman Leeson's Roberta Breitmore series and Kate Craig-Wood's website iwanttobeagirl.org, which I find highly problematic for its focus on the "normal" and its absolute endorsement of surgery. I think of this as a performance of indecision, which for a transgender person facing the medical/legal/ psychiatric nexus of power, is the one thing we're never supposed to show. The piece is also a performance of a more genderqueer perspective, with deep reservations and concerns about surgery as the preferred option for trans people.

virus.circus.laboratory

virus.circus.laboratory is an episode of *virus.circus* in the form of an alternative reality installation of the laboratory of the DIY medical resistance within our slipstream non-linear narrative. The lab projects memory recordings of past futures from previous episodes in the form of video, sound, biometric data and interactive electronics. Consisting of an episodic series of performances and installations using wearable electronics, soft sensors and live audio to bridge virtual and physical spaces, the performances explore queer futures of latex sexuality and DIY medicine amidst a speculative world of virus hysteria. The history of queer politics shows that the rhetoric of viruses such as HIV are used to control marginalized populations, while viruses such as H1N1 reproduce these structures of power. *virus.circus* follows the viral as a transversal line of inquiry that intersects with the militarization of medical authority, microscopic transnational migrations and global economic inequality.

http://transreal.org

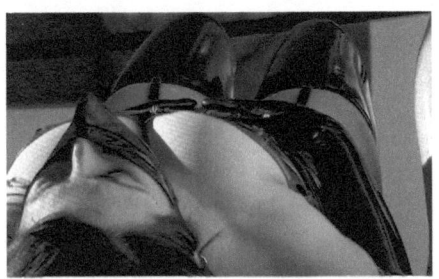
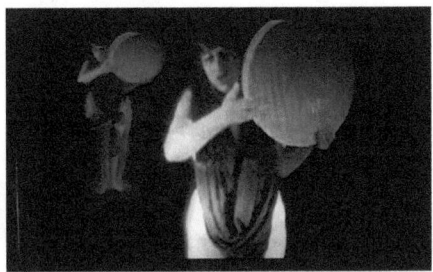

Elle Mehrmand is a performance artist and musician who uses the body, electronics, video, sound and installation within her work. She is the singer and trombone player of Assembly of Mazes, a music collective who creates dark, electronic, middle eastern, rhythmic jazz rock. Elle is currently an MFA candidate at UCSD, and received her BFA in art photography with a minor in music at CSULB. She is a collective member of the Electronic Disturbance Theatre 2.0 and the b.a.n.g. Lab, and is a researcher at CRCA ←Center for Research and Computing in the Arts→ at UCSD. Her work has been internationally shown at venues such as Los Angeles Contemporary Exhibitions ←LACE→, the Museum of Contemporary Art San Diego ←MCASD→, Highways Performance Space, Orange County Museum of Art ←OCMA→, UCLA Freud Playhouse, CECUT, the Nevada Museum of Art, and the Gallery of the Nat'l College of Art and Design. She has been discussed in Artforum, Art21, the LA Times, Juxtapoz Magazine, WIRED, Networked Performance, the LA & OC Weekly, Furtherfield.org, the CityBeat, and VICE magazine.

wiki-abmeyad addresses the issues of diasporic subjects, transnational politics, and the relationship between art and science through the use of digital cloning and sensing technologies. In this ritualistic performance Mehrmand sings wikileaks cables about Iran in Farsi and English with a Persian daf drum and an ironic headscarf from American Apparel. The holographic performance of her digitized clone, enacts the split subject to explore diaspora as fragmentation, dis/location and fractures within spaces, while terrorizing and subverting a traditionally militarized use of technology. The CO2 sensor in the space is connected to the audio program Pure Data, adding more echo to the sound as more viewers enter the space, complicating the passive gaze of the viewer/participant. Wiki-abmeyad continues Mehrmand's research on organic interfaces for music making, expanding on the use of the body as an instrument to include the temporal and spatial relationships between bodies and machines.

virus.circus follows the viral as a transversal line of inquiry that intersects with the militarization of medical authority, microscopic transnational migrations and global economic inequality. Consisting of an episodic series of performances using wearable electronics, soft sensors and live audio to bridge virtual and physical spaces, the performances explore queer futures of latex sexuality and DIY medicine amidst a speculative world of virus hysteria. The history of queer politics shows that the rhetoric of viruses such as HIV are used to control marginalized populations, while viruses such as H1N1 reproduce these structures of power.

http://elleelleelle.org
http://www.assemblyofmazes.com

Michael Kontopoulos

WATER RITES

Robert Heinlein's celebrated 1961 novel, *Stranger in a Strange Land*, tells the story of a human baby that is marooned on Mars and raised by native Martians. Upon his return to Earth, he must acclimatize to human culture and customs, including the cavalier relationship that humans have to water. On his native Mars, an arid planet, the sharing of water with another person is a ceremonial gesture which, when completed, cements the two individuals together with the new and sacred title of "water brother". Science fiction provides many such examples of encounters between disparate cultures, usually exacerbated by differences in resource management or law. Few of them address, with such solemnity and rigor, the extent to which the extreme scarcity of water – a resource most of us take for granted – can produce and encode such morally-ordered social interactions. Another example from literature is given in Frank Herbert's *Dune* (1965), where certain curious social gestures develop on the arid fictional planet of Arackis to show respect, such as spitting at the feet of another person in lieu of hand-shaking (as an offering of your inner water to them).

Speculative fictional gestures, such as this hold a mirror to our own culture. They ask us to question our own relationship to water. Consider the hydrology of our planet: Earth boasts 1.34 billion cubic kilometers of water. 96% of that water is salty and undrinkable. 70% of the remaining fresh water is frozen in ice-caps. Most of the remainder is only available as moisture or is hidden in aquifers too deep for humans to reach. Ultimately, less than 1% of the water on Earth is potable and available for human use.[1] This water is mostly found in lakes, rivers and accessible underground aquifers. A marginal amount of this water is sustainable–regularly renewed via the natural hydrologic cycle. And yet, human demands on fresh water are increasing at completely unsustainable rates, to accommodate people's consumption needs, but also for many manufacturing and industry needs. To further complicate matters, the population of the Earth is expected to increase dramatically by 2052 and the climate is warming and destabilizing. 'Water' occupies an ambiguous territory between a public trust and a private commodity which is metered, monitored and distributed by governing bodies, depending on the needs of the region. Every country is at work, trying to prevent water crises in their region by investing in new methods of water management and treatment.

Now consider California alone. In California, we face enormous challenges adapting our inefficient water management system to contemporary

---

1   Igor Shiklomanov (1993), Peter H. Gleick, ed., World fresh water resources, in *Water in Crisis: A Guide to the World's Fresh Water Resources*, Oxford University Press, pp. 13–24

2   "International Data Base (IDB) — World Population". Census.gov. 2010-06-28. Retrieved 2010-08-01.

conditions. The state continues to grow and urbanize, and it is thirsty. Most of Southern California's water is imported via several of the state's surface water conveyance systems, including the State Water Project, the LA Aqueduct and the Colorado River delivery systems. Groundwater is also being pumped at unsustainable rates in some regions. Conveyance systems are susceptible to long periods of drought, making water scarcity an occasional reality. The frailty of Southern California's water situation is encapsulated in the management of the Sacramento-San Juaquin Delta. If the delta's weak levees were to fail in a large earthquake, for example, the region would be flooded with salt water. A huge percentage of Los Angeles' water supply would be cut off for months or even years.[3] Urban water-use efficiency and reclamation methods are improving, but still, major infrastructural changes are necessary to prevent cataclysmic disturbances in LA's water supply (not to mention the environmental and agricultural impact).

It is not outrageous to imagine a merging of the contemporary urban landscape of Los Angeles with the elaborate water-sharing ceremonies of Heinlein's *Stranger in a Strange Land*, or Herbert's *Dune*. Los Angeles has always been a locus for a wide variety of communes, "intentional commu-

3   Ellen Hanak, Jay Lund, Ariel Dinar, Brian Gray, Richard Howitt, Jeffrey Mount, Peter Moyle, Barton "Buzz" Thompson, *Managing California's Water From Conflict to Reconciliation*, San Francisco: Public Policy Institute of California, 2011

nities" and alternative spiritualities. The unique geography and liberal urban ethos of the city have always nurtured this disposition. The history of the city is peppered with examples such as those of the Source Family or the Nature Boys as well as scores of bohemian and beatnik enclaves. On a more casual scale, one can observe the increasing adoption of spiritual practices into secular life – if only to reap the health benefits. Yoga, meditation and vegan/vegetarian lifestyles are just a few simple examples of such 'civil religion' practices. Consider this openness to new spiritualities in context, i.e., with Los Angeles' growing austerity and conservation efforts around urban water use and reclamation. It is challenging enough for people to accept changes in the status quo or be forced to change their habits, giving up activities or ways of living and acting which they are accustomed to. One can imagine a situation in which pseudo-spiritual rituals evolve to celebrate or consecrate water. That assumption is the point of departure for this work.

Water Rites addresses the social response to the diminishing quantity of a resource. Following the logic of Heinlein or Herbert, when something is scarce it becomes culturally precious. Making, moving and most notably, sharing it, carries with it a heightened social significance in the moral order. The piece is comprised of four DIY devices that are partially electronic (two mobile water-purifying devices, one "altar" and one tool for communal drinking), and a two-channel video installation. Each channel follows one of two individuals—presumably romantic partners—as they prepare a water source for a specific ceremony. The ceremony combines many of the common stages found in religious and secular rituals. These include, but are not limited to the establishment of an *intention*, the defining of a *sacred space*, the *invocation* of greater energies, *concretion* of a substance, washing, *cleansing* and ultimately, conclusion of the ceremony by recounting the initial intention and leaving the space with an *offering*. The main purpose of the ceremony is for the two individuals to engage in an act of bonding using water. The decision to combine water sources and drink together is a symbolic act that codifies their relationship and gives it meaning. It is left intentionally ambiguous whether or not this is a ceremony that has been practiced by many people over many years, or simply something these two people invented together that has special meaning only to them. In the end, one might ponder: Is this implying a dystopian vision of Los Angeles, considering our current trajectory of poor water management? Could this be ushering us into an alternative present? Perhaps a more appropriate question to ask is: Why would it be *surprising* if such a practice existed today?

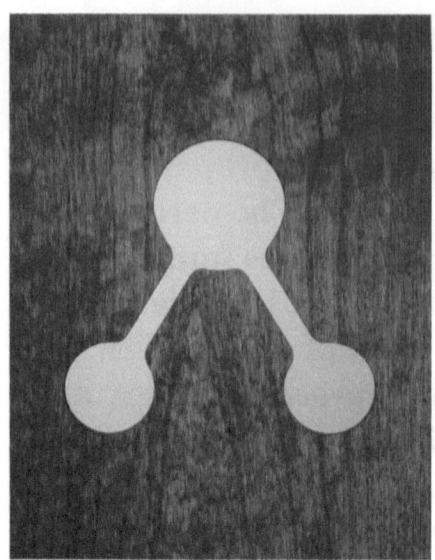

I have always approached art as a wayward anthropologist. I feel I am constantly involved in a process of "participant observation" in the everyday world. Though an artist, I pretend I am a historian of the everyday; of nuanced, solitary gestures and complex social entanglements. Thematically, I am interested in stories that DIY objects and electronic devices can tell us about the people who use them and the world they employ them in. The deployment of an electronic system or machine represents a response to a specific need. But what happens when no device exists to address one's needs? The underlying assumption of all my work is that in such a case, a person will exercise his/her agency and invent their own. As the artist, I tell the story of that person.

When conceiving of my work, I draw heavily on tropes and strategies in science fiction as well as in modern cosmology. Notably, I am influenced by the idea of 'a-temporality' or, at least, of possible transgressions of temporality: suggestions of a potential future, or glimpses at an alternative present. A less inhibited term for science fiction is "speculative fiction" because more often than not, a propositional reality is a vehicle by which to critique elements of our living, codified reality. I aspire to similar ends, but through the invention and documentation of objects. I am a speculative inventor.

My actual process conflates several methods. To start, I value the role of rigor in art-making. Research, iterative development and skepticism are essential to my practice. I am also interested in craft and form, as it is informed by contemporary technological affordances. I am interested in the aesthetics of DIY and the creative problem-solving capacity of ordinary individuals. Like a pendulum, my methodology oscillates between two points: rigorous research into my chosen theme, and the invention of diegetic prototypes by which one can investigate that theme. In an exhibition, I typically display objects alongside a video exploration of that object. In the end, my goal is to imagine (and call into question) the circumstances under which that object may exist. Who made it and for what reason? Under what conditions of social want?; A want that catalyzed their invention of this prototype. I strive to ask these questions through the work I present, by blending the narrative and the mimetic; showing and telling, though never enforcing.

Michael Kontopoulos is a Los Angeles based artist and educator. After studying electronic and time-based Art at Carnegie Mellon University, he went on to receive his MFA in Design and Media Arts from UCLA. He has exhibited solo and collaborative projects in galleries, festivals and conferences in the U.S., Asia and Europe, including the Santa Monica Glow Festival, the Sundance Film Festival, and the TED conference. He was the winner of a 2010 Rhizome Commission for emerging artists, sponsored by the New Museum (NYC). Currently, Michael teaches electronic media courses at USC and Cal State Long Beach.

http://www.mkontopoulos.com

Video Credits:
Christopher O'Leary (Photographer)
Michael Kontopoulos (Director, Editor)
Yiannis Christofides (Composer)
Marcela Coto (Assistant Director)

Starring:
Johanna Reed
Mattia Casalegno

Special Thanks:
Steven Joyner and Machine Histories
James Cerasani
Pieter, PASD
Dr. Ellen Hanack
Marcela Coto

Xárene Eskandar

ARCHITECTURAL ORGANS

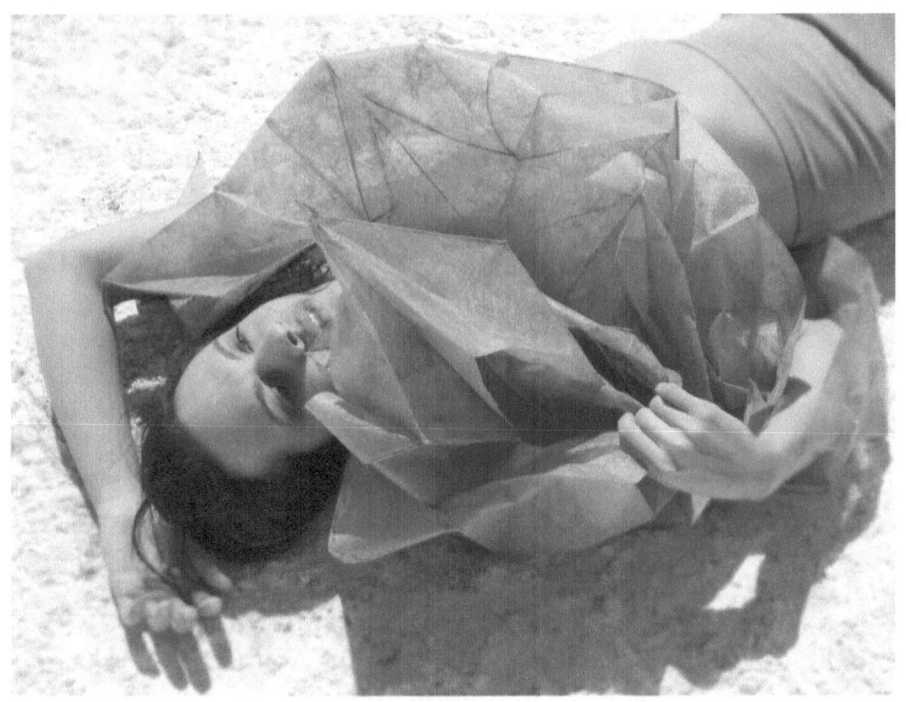

By using three keywords that Marcos Novak's concept of
Transvergence is situated upon—ontology, immanence and allo—
I began questioning *what is* to find the response *this is*. What
is being? What is becoming? What is other? I follow this with
"What if?". "What if?" is the question of the speculative; it is what
transforms the philosopher's "What is?" to the scientist's "This
is." My work, therefore, should not be mistaken for a utopia only
latent with "What ifs"; it is the process of "tomorrow" becoming
"now." In this quest I have homed in on the fold and its potential
for developing new possibilities for modes of existence and
occupation of space, in the form of *architectural organs*—origami-
like extensions of our body; an actual organ of skin. Where are
fold (n.) and folding (v.) positioned as responses to these questions
and speculations of change? Why a fold? What is a fold anyway?

To fold is to hide; to unfold is to reveal; a fold therefore,
holds both opposite actions (hiding and revealing) within one
dimension of the fold line. Spatially, the area where my interest
lies in, the one-dimensionality of the line reveals and hides
the capability of two-dimensional planes becoming a three-
dimensional form. A fold is a multiple of potentials waiting to be
realized. Therefore, a fold, a Deleuzian being-as-becoming, the
line-as-plane-as-form, exists on a plane of immanence, latent with
possibilities. The key to existing on this plane is desire. Folding is
the act of including and excluding, of containing both the inside
and the outside, this and that. One desires to fold and unfold,
or in other words, to pursue potentials. Italo Calvino's city of
Chloé best illustrates the desire of the potential, what Rosetta
Di Pace-Jordan explains as the "dynamism latent in all matter",
and in Chloé, the dynamism latent in all relationships. Chloé
both includes thousands of possible relationships between its
inhabitants, as well as excluding them—the well-being of the city
based on the exclusion, or folding-in and leaving out, rather than
un-folding and playing out.

A fold, or a *ptychosis*, as applied in medical English, is the behavior of becoming something other. A single becoming the double, becoming the multiple, exemplified in embryonic folding, where each fold yields another part to the single disk of the organism, multiplying its parts by continually folding over itself. This process is that of a machinic phylum, where folding of heterogeneous parts–ectoderm (outside) and endoderm (inside)– creates a new entity. In origami, just as in embryonic folding, the combinations of transverse and longitudinal folds arrive at different forms. However, different from embryonic folding, origami has a homogenous base, which through a dynamic process ends in a static form. In Latin, fold (v.) and arrive (v.) are both plico, an active tense. Once a fold arrives at a point, that point should only become a departure point to another form.

We are continuously experiencing series of arrivals and departures at and from points; our lives are broken into milestones and anniversaries. We are in a constant mode of unfolding and changing, our single body becoming multiples in the compounded unfolding of its future. Our body is therefore analogous to the fold. However, we go through this dynamic process with a static, homogenous base: our body. So the question now shifts from *what is a fold*, to how can a folded form (our body departing and arriving at various points in space-time) continue embodying the dynamism that initially created it? How can our bodies become a machinic phylum for the realization of architectural organs? What are the heterogeneities that must be synthesized?

INDUSTRIAL ECOLOGY TO SOCIAL ECOLOGY TO ANARCHIC ECOLOGY

We are on course for the realization of architectural organs. Over the last 150 years, our relationship with technology has shifted focus from production at any cost, to human-centered design, to environmentally conscious design. The final step is a shift to a fragmented and sustainable, autonomous design, a shift which has already begun.

Charlie Chaplin's *Modern Times* is a seminal piece of the folding of the human *into* technology, the first machinic phylum of modern times. Filmed in 1936, it is the futuristic and extended vision of the events set off a century earlier with the second Industrial Revolution and the introduction of factory modernization to the domestic realm. This is a period when the technology takes precedence over the human, where production came at any cost to the environment; child labour was rampant, and worker rights were unheard of. The deep red sky and smoke stacks of Monet's paintings are not romantic reminiscing of the city, but factual impressions of the coal grime across the landscape and lives of citizens. Like Chaplin's film, Fritz Lange's *Metropolis* (1927) is created at the height of Scientific Management: The machinic efficiency of the human body, not for the benefit of the human, but for the production of profit–the "economic efficiency" of Taylorism— better put, the efficient production of an economy of profit at the expense of the human worker. Christine Fredrick's *Scientific Management of the Home*, by introducing the concept of efficiency for the female worker in her duties of housework, completes the cycle of profit production, with profit consumption.

There is a contrarian shift within the same time-period, of efficiency becoming more human centered. Frank and Lilian Gilbreth, inspired by Taylor's work focus on the production of efficiency towards the production of welfare: a folding of the human *onto* technology. In their scenario, the human is still part of the machine, but the process of production is not at the cost of the human. This shift of focus hastens through the mid-century as more human elements are folded onto the technology, arriving at the second machinic phylum and Henry Dreyfus' *Designing for Humans* (1955) which sets the standards for the study of human factors: the sensibility and attention to the human element of technology, where humans are not the heterogeneous parts of a factory, but as in Marshall McLuhan's terms, the mechanical technology becomes an extension of the human body.

This folding and re-folding of the human and technology has unfolded itself to a flat sheet of creases, ready to be re-folded with new terms: the environment. Once resolving the relationship of the mechanic modernization with the human, our focus shifted to the well-being of the human environment, Earth. We realize we have enveloped her in the same archaic ways as when we were enveloped by the machines of industrialization. In *Social Ecology and Revolutionary Thought*, Murray Bookchin points out that the dysfunctional relationship between human and nature stems from the dysfunctional relationship between humans, "To state this thought more precisely: the imbalances man has produced in the natural world are caused by the imbalances he has produced in the social world."

The point of view of this essay is completely Western. In China, unfortunately, factory citizens are the inhabitants of corporate cities, perhaps, one can say, true integration of human into machine. Therefore, it is naive to say that our shift in focus to the environment means we have resolved the social imbalances; it only acknowledges them. We exist on two parallel dimensions: one where we still exist within the first machinic phylum, the other where with much struggle we pretend to have moved out of it but in reality we have not, because we consume it.

As we continue to fold in and out of the creases of the past to find new folds for our future, we have come upon the third machinic phylum, the *folding of technology onto the human*. Here we are tearing into two separate, yet related paths: the use of mobile technologies as prosthesis, and the expansion of embedded networks, a tethered prosthesis of the human to nature, and a reversal of *our* embedding into the factory. Whereas a century ago Scientific Management made the human—to its detriment—more efficient for the production of profit, embedded networks, through activating nature, make it more efficient in the production of knowledge for its own sake. Embedded systems also activate architecture by folding in multiple layers of interaction between systems—the systems of the different operators of the space and the bodies occupying it.

"With every tool man is perfecting his own organs, whether motor or sensory, or is removing the limits to their functioning. Motor power places gigantic forces at his disposal, which, like his muscles, he can employ in any direction... and the dwelling-house was a substitute for the mother's womb, the first lodging, for which in all likelihood man still longs, and in which he was safe and felt at ease. [...] Man has, as it were, become a prosthetic god. When he puts on all his auxiliary organs he is truly magnificent; but those organs have not grown onto him and they still give him much trouble at times."   —Sigmund Freud, *Civilization and its Discontents*, 1930, pp 42-43.

For sixteen years Freud suffered from the pain of a prosthetic jaw and palate, put in place as a result of cancer. His prosthesis was placed *onto* him, rather than, as he writes in this self-reflective piece, "*grown onto* him." At some point, the heterogeneities of human and technology, having switched forces repeatedly over time, eventually find equilibrium. This will be the fourth machinic phylum: the *folding of technology and human into each other*. This is the point where technology is no longer a prosthetic, where metaphors of architecture as prosthesis for nature or body no longer hold true. This is when, as Arakawa and Gins arrive at, that we become Architectural Bodies, a reconfiguration of the organism-person-surround.

We are, however, debilitated through our own history and stopped dead in our tracks. Archaic notions of beauty, narrow views on gender, misconceptions of race, and misunderstandings of philosophies of existence, must be re-evaluated through a process of unfolding, meaning that every scenario should be allowed to play out in order to evaluate its effects on our progress: every idea of beauty, every variation on gender; every identification and valuation of self and not others, with reference to an empirical religion.

Model: Karis Wilde
Production Assistant: Joanna Cheung
Animation: Thomas Williams
Audio & Video: Xárene Eskandar

Xárene Eskandar is a researcher and designer with a diverse background ranging from fashion and automotive design to architecture and live audio-visuals. She holds a Bachelor of Science in Design from University of Cincinnati, Department of Design, Architecture, Art and Planning, her MFA from Design Media Arts, UCLA, and is currently working on her PhD in Media Arts and Technology, UCSB.

Drawing upon cultural anthropology, her research is focused on the evolution of the symbiotic relationship of technology and the human with the aim of creating crossover points into dimensions and ecologies referred to as 'utopia', whether technological, architectural or social. Her interest lies in questions that debunk prescriptions within either of these categories, and to instead offer neolexia for our future hybrid bodies.

She is an avid collector of books, sand and cat whiskers.

http://www.xarene.com
http://tentativearchitecture.net

Pinar Yoldas

THREE
PERSPECTIVES
ON A
FUTURE OF
INTIMACY

Imagine an enormous fish tank embedded in a wall.

The water in it is murky with leaf skeletons and brown particles floating around.

You walk towards it.

There's some light coming from behind. Hard to tell whether it's the afternoon sunlight or some florescent aquarium lighting.

As you walk towards it you notice some blurry shadows move, perhaps fish, but then something else moves...something...

...big.

You get closer. Nervous? Yeah. But you can't stop. You need to know what's in that pool of filthy biomass.

It's drawing you in.

Put your hand on the glass. It feels warm. Some bubbles move up leaving a trail right where you placed your hand.

You wait.

A woman comes out of the murk.

A woman is in the tank. A kind of woman. Freakishly feminine.

Her voluptuous breasts are bare, bouncing like two balloons filled with milk as she presses them against the glass, exactly where your hand is.

You step back in total shock, your eyes still glued to her breasts. As you look at this beautiful torso of a mermaid, a spicy blend of fear and desire pours onto you. Her perfectly shaped pink nipples and pale skin contrasts with the burnt ochre water in the tank. She moves up, her breasts gently shaking in a most inviting way...

That's exactly when you notice that she has more than two of them. You are torn between screaming and running away or staying in place.

You choose to stay.

You first see four boobs, then six, then twelve--all of them achingly swollen, round, ripe and radiant. As she--at this point, you're sure it's not a woman in the traditional sense, but it's okay to call her a "she"--slithers her body against the glass of the tank, you see more and more boobs attached to her serpentine body.

You lose count; she has more than a hundred, perhaps a thousand. Regardless, you know you've never seen this many naked boobs at once before.

You wonder how deep this tank could be to host that many boobs. What you would call "sexual arousal" five minutes ago before "she" started flashing her multiple tits at you is now replaced by an alert but calm aftershock. Like what you felt the first time you saw a real crocodile in the zoo when you were five.

As you're thinking these thoughts she moves away from the glass and gradually fades out in the vagueness of the cloudy waters, taking her many many boobs with her.

Now that the spectacle is over, you're left by the fish tank with your own heartbeat (which has become quite audible) and the same brown particles floating around in the same unexciting way they did before "she" showed up.

You just met SuperMammal.

#2

SuperMammal is one of our biggest synbio projects thanks to a very generous budget from our sponsors.

It's also the most, how do you say it, ethically controversial, and the most exciting.

Controversy and excitement always go hand in hand, I guess. When we first started three years ago, we had no idea that the project would become so big, I mean, literally.

Now the SuperMammal can reach up to 200 segments, a very striking number indeed. It weighs up to, let me think, each segment is about the 1/5th of an average human, so it'd be 150 divided by 5 multiplied by 200, 6000 pounds!!! Hmm...I don't think she weighs that much though; I mean, she's leaner maybe, around 4200? Ugh, I'll ask my assistant about that later if you need accurate numbers for your copy.

When our very first clients approached us, we were hesitant to take on this project.

First off, we weren't sure which path to take.

One option was to fabricate it in vitro cell by cell, tissue by tissue. The other option was to design the entire genome from scratch, which basically translates to...designing a new species. Some call it playing God, but that's not the case.

As human beings, we're not the fastest or the strongest, nor the most intelligent. But we're the best in transforming what's around us for our own good. We've been manipulating both the living and the non-living. We carve holes into mountains. We build SUVs.

We harness nuclear power. And we've been extracting chemicals from other species since the beginning of history. We modify molecules, we heat them, cool them down, mix them etc...DNA is just another molecule.

In that sense, it's no difference than making wine from grapes and cheese from milk for the sake of tickling our taste buds. Why make wine? Why make cheese? Okay, we somehow made these, but why eat them together? Why go on a wine and cheese tasting cruise to some five star resort in Portugal?

Why?

Because...it feels good!

You tickle the taste buds more; you stimulate them so much that they scream at your brain: "Initiate pleasure! Now!"

Human beings will not stop until pleasure is initiated.

The concept of SuperMammal is no exception. The main difference being that SM can tickle more than just your oral senses.

It is a brand new species of excess. An excess of sexuality, so to speak.

I'd like to be honest with you, our first prototype of the female SuperMammal was not very successful in arousing sexual desire. We made her breasts swollen, creamy and smooth; we made them soft and full; we made them throbbing with need. Gestalt psychology says the whole is greater than the sum of its parts. We proved the exact opposite. The whole was much less attractive than each single breast segment. At least to the majority. There were a few testers who did like SM #1. They would suck on her breasts until her nipples started bleeding.

Anyway, that's another story...

The next one was a big success. The male SM. The ultimate perpetual erection machine. We had to rush a couple of those as they instantly became the most sought-after sex animal of VIP orgies. You can think of the male SM as a sexual arousal hub; you plug into it (it plugs into you to be morphologically correct), and it connects you to others...

Building on that same idea, we went onto design the male/female SM. A bricolage of male and female genitalia. Can host all kinds of bodies with all kinds of tendencies. It got particularly popular, for it enhances user interaction. It can be penetrated and penetrate at the same time. It was another phenomenal success.

Now it s reported that some users forced male/female SM to penetrate itself, naively thinking that little SM s would pop out after nine months. But SM doesn t work that way.

SM play is not a reproductive process. It is a seductive, excessive process.

#3

Supermammal is a uniquely personal experience. At first, I was shy to try it . When my friend called me on a warm summer afternoon about this SM party, my response was harsh: "What kind of zoophiliac perverts are you guys? Collectively fucking a freak of nature?"

I was downright wrong.

I think I needed an excuse to override my prejudices about pain and pleasure.
To be more specific: genetically engineered pleasure.

My boyfriend leaving me due to sexual incompatibilities--it takes more than a hole and a stick for a successful sex life--was the out I desperately needed. For I had, as a middle-aged woman who worried about her sexually active years slipping away one by one, decided to try anything and everything.

My quest in life became to understand what sex is and why (or how) it is done. I was as purposeful as an arrow leaving its bow. I was gonna start with the most extreme of sexual extremities: A SuperMammal Slide.

It is called a slide since each person has to slide from one segment of the SM to another. Whoever finishes every segment of the animal first, gets the big prize.

The Slide was one of the most challenging SM games out there, since it required copious amounts of copulation. Although I knew I wasn' endowed with such stamina, I decided to give it a shot.

I thought to myself, if I can survive this, I can survive anything (or 55% of those other things on my to do list).

The big day came. I grabbed my organic lubricant and my energy drink and went to see SuperMammal.

The first thought: It is big.

The second thought: It is disgusting.

The third thought: What the heck am I doing here?

Although I had seen pictures of SM before, I was nowhere close to being prepared .

I picked up my lubricant and energy drink and headed towards the door. A tall young gentleman with nerdy glasses who saw me leaving stopped me. Tightly holding my shoulder, he said: " I know what you're thinking. Trust me, it is a uniquely personal experience, and you'll regret it if you miss out on it." I said, "Okay," in a squeaky thin voice trembling in shock upon the sight of SM.

The Slide begins with a "warm up," which involves caressing the animal, fondling its organs and touching or kissing each other. Then one by one, we started sitting on it.

After everybody was plugged in, we started a rhythmic wave of hip movements, pulsating in unison with lukewarm, tender pleasure.

We kept going like that for about eight minutes, then we started "sliding"--each person moving up to sit on the next segment with the person in the foremost segment going to the back, etc. Crazy, huh?

I should say I was stunned by how "human" the skin-to-skin experience felt.

SuperMammal was pleasantly warm and nice inside me and oddly enough I could feel its other penises move in other people. I could feel its many vaginas gradually expand and contract. It was serving all of us at once, silently, unifying us under the same sensation.

Once upon a time, a dance teacher I had told me that life is nothing but rhythm. I hadn't given it much thought then, as I have a tendency to shut down during dance and yoga classes the moment I detect the slightest hint of new agey blabber.

Under this new light of being hooked up to a SM, as I undulated with some twenty other people, I realized what she meant.

My thighs were shaking with the rhythm of its multiple genitalia. My heart was beating to the rhythm of its many hearts. My mind stained by the queer color of intimacy, I felt something about me which I would like to call "my soul," ripple with the rhythm of its synapses.

Not some fancy plastic sex toy, not an animal, definitely not a human, its mere presence defied all the known categories of life and being.

Closely attached to its nervous system, I closed my eyes, melting in an alien bliss of interspecies love.

I had no choice but to accept SuperMammal.

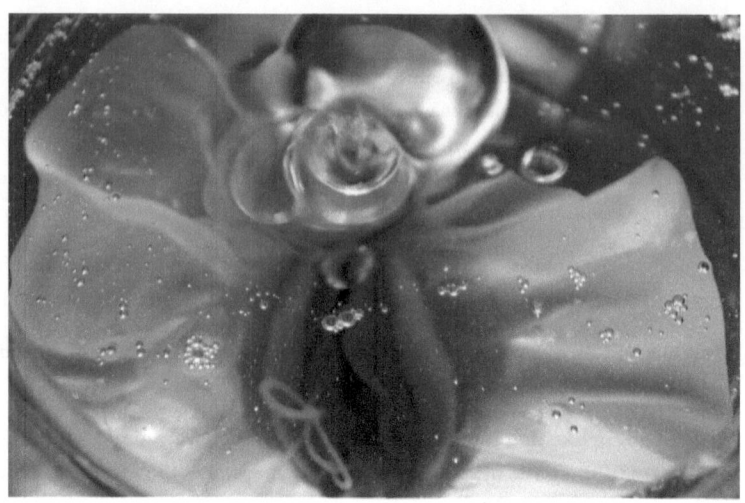

According to Deleuze and Guattari, philosophy, science and art are approaches to **chaos** that attempt to bring order to it . Art creates sensations, science creates functions, and philosophy creates concepts in order to frame **chaos**.

Born and raised in a highly unstable part of the world (economically, politically, culturally) where instability was steadily maintained thanks to the effects of events such as the 1981 military coup, 1985 chernobyl nuclear disaster, Iran-Iraq war, Gulf War, all sorts of terrorist attacks, and finally, the radical Islamic movement of the last decade, tocount a few, I have an innate tendency to perceive life as chaos and categories of life as chaotic systems. Hence, as an artist, I'm most interested in the intersection of art, science and philosophy, and my art/theory practice is the manifestation of my diverse interests in each of these fields.

Jack Burnham says: "A systems viewpoint is focused on the creation of stable, on-going relationships between organic and nonorganic systems, be these neighborhoods, industrial complexes, farms, transportation systems, information centers, recreation centers, or any of the other matrices of human activity."

I'm particularly focused on sociocultural systems in regards to biological systems. Again, approaching "matrices of human activity" as dynamic systems that heavily effect natural phenomena, I direct my gaze at "critical moments" where chaotic behavior emerges out of the encounters between "culture" and "nature."

Throughout my past work, I have explored these critical moments: moments of intensity, moments of dynamic exchange, moments of change and transformation. In *Scream: A Homage to Edward Munch and All the Dead Racoons* (2008), the impact of US presidential elections on our blue planet is discussed through a harshly visceral interface that examines the interchange between the political and biological. In *Shock Therapy* (2010), a smart wearable device recognizes the act of shopping and hijacks the consumer's physical body to elaborately stage a conflict between the somatosensory system and the prefrontal cortex . In *Limbique* (2010), the tangible and spatial aspects of the human brain, which gives rise to the intangible and the volumeless, are visualized. In *Fabula* (2008), global sites of waste as highly dynamic nonorganic systems that show chaotic behavior pose the possibility of sentient life forms emerging from such man made extreme environments.

There are very tight bonds between our nervous systems and our technologically driven society. I try to reveal these connections to trigger a new understanding of the body and its environment.

Pinar Yoldas is a Turkish artist, designer, neuro-enthusiast. Building on her varied background in art, architecture and science, her work is a series of multi-modal experiments on the human sensorium. Lately, she has been designing synthetic biological systems as a living critique of our society. Pinar has a BArch from METU , MS from ITU , MA from Istanbul Bilgi University and an MFA from UCLA. Her residencies include the MacDowell Colony, UCross foundation, VCCA, Duke University and University of Minnesota.

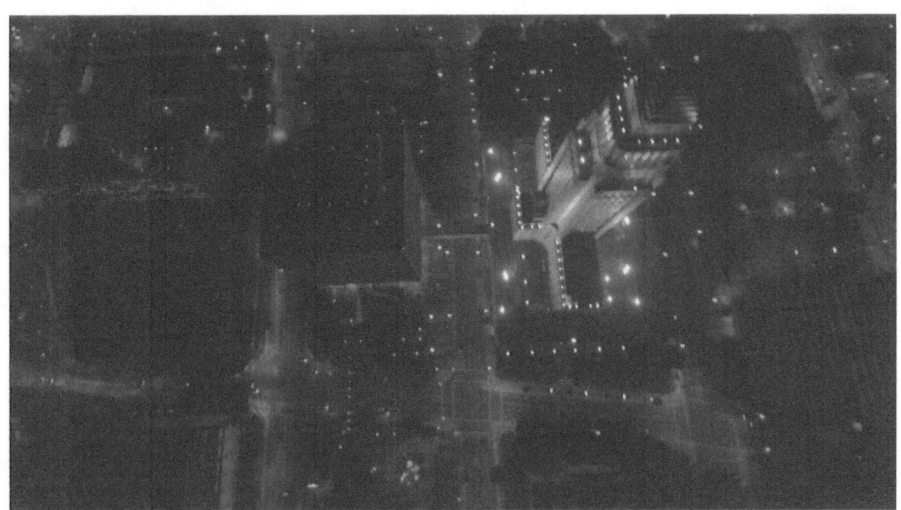

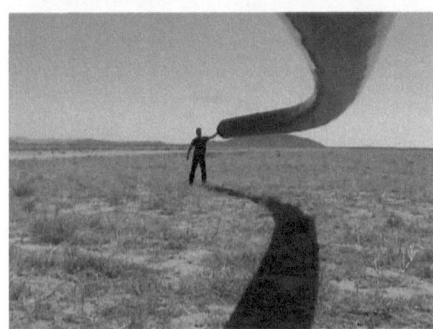

Jeff Cain is an artist and designer who works with sculpture, video, sound, photography, and performance. His studio, the Shed Research Institute, is an umbrella organization for independent research, public art projects, and site-specific design projects. Cain received his MFA in studio art from Cal Arts. His works have been shown at the Musee d'art Modern de Ville de Paris and Kyiv's Center for Contemporary Art, as well as locally at the Getty Museum, Los Angeles County Museum of Art, UCI University Art Gallery, Track 16, and the 18th Street Arts Center.

Cain's work was written about in the Getty's catalog *California Video*, SoCCAS' book *The Aesthetics of Risk*, and in *Art in America*. His writing has been published in *Art Journal* and numerous exhibition catalogs and online journals.

Cain has made several radio based projects, including, a project that decodes the LAPD digital radio and rebroadcasts it on the LAPD's original AM station, and a broadcast radio technology called RHZ Radio that is a hybrid online and broadcast infrastructure that techno-logically obeys the FCC broadcast law but allows legal neighborhood radio stations without a permit. RHZ Radio was nominated for the Prix Ars Electronica in 2005.

He has worked as faculty at USC Roski School of Fine Arts, CalArts, Cal State Fullerton, Sci-Arc, and Whittier College.

http://shedresearch.net

www.ingramcontent.com/pod-product-compliance
Lightning Source LLC
Chambersburg PA
CBHW022017170526
45157CB00003B/1270